THE PATH TO YOUR HOME
A Practical Guide to Home Buying
⣿ GAYE NEWTON ⣿

Galibren
Written Treasures®

GALIBREN WRITTEN TREASURES, LLC

Arlington, Virginia | www.galibren.com

The Path to Your Home: A Practical Guide to Home Buying
by Gaye Newton

Published by Galibren Written Treasures, LLC
P.O. Box 7644, Arlington, VA 22207
www.galibren.com

This book is for general reference and is intended as practical advice. It is not a substitute for advice from legal, financial, real estate, and other related professionals. The author and publisher disclaim any personal liability, directly or indirectly, for advice or information presented within. Although the author and publisher have made every effort to ensure the accuracy and appropriateness of the information included, we assume no responsibility for error, inaccuracies, omissions, or inconsistencies. For major decisions affecting your life and your own home buying experience, consult legal, financial, and real estate professionals.

Cover and design by Sagetopia, LLC
Cover photograph by David Papazian

First Printing 2005
Printed in the United States of America

1   3   5   7   9   10   8   6   4   2

Publisher's Cataloging-in-Publication
(Provided by Quality Books, Inc.)

Newton, Gaye.
    The path to your home : a practical guide to home
buying / Gaye Newton.
    p. cm.
    Includes index.
    LCCN 2004098883
    ISBN 0-9700849-1-9

    1. House buying.   I. Title.

TH4817.5.N49 2005   643'.12
                          QBI04-200526

ABOUT THE AUTHOR

Gaye Newton is an author and the owner of Galibren Written Treasures, LLC, a business and creative writing services company. She received a bachelor's degree in psychology from Oberlin College and master's degrees in management and psychology from Purdue University. Her publications include novel *Past Presence*, poetry, and song lyrics on the compact disc *Happy Together* by the Lafayette Harris, Jr. Trio featuring Melba Moore.

Gaye has owned five homes, encompassing four states, three resales, two new constructions, and a lifetime supply of address change forms. She currently resides in the Washington, D.C. area in House #5.

Also by Gaye Newton
Past Presence

ACKNOWLEDGEMENTS

I must first give special thanks to the eleven experts who contributed to this book and helped bring it to life: Art Auerbach, Gail Belt, Susan Corcoran, Emory Hackman, Jean Keller, Kevin Mahoney, Lilian Rodriguez, Lou Scerbo, Sue van der Linden, Jason Werther, and Jonna Wooten. I also wish to thank Sung Hee Kim and David Papazian for their creativity, Cynthia Robertson and Susan Corcoran for their unique points of view, Hilary Cumberton for her eye for detail, and my editor, Karyn Langhorne Wynn.

Finally, I must thank my family for passing on the tradition of home ownership. Long ago there actually was a time in my life when I lived in one house for more than three years. I pass to the next generation my father's sage advice: "Never miss a mortgage payment!"

For everyone who's ever dreamed of crossing the threshold of that very first house.

TABLE OF CONTENTS

1

YOU KNOW IT'S TIME TO BUY A HOUSE WHEN...

You're tired of paying rent. You need an extra bedroom for the newest baby. You're getting a job transfer. Something smaller sounds good now that the kids have moved out. You just want a place that's all yours. The reasons are easy. The decision to go ahead is exciting. But a house is probably one of the most complicated purchases you'll ever make.

If you've purchased a car, you know there are several steps to take: decide what you need, choose a model and features, get financing, and drive that baby off the lot. Buying that car is like wanting a cheeseburger, going to the store to buy ingredients, then bringing them home to prepare. It takes a little time, planning and effort, but in the end, you'll have your cheeseburger.

But buying a house is a lot more involved. This time when you want that cheeseburger, you go outside and plant wheat, lettuce, and tomatoes. Then you raise some cattle. And while you're waiting for your homemade cheese to age, you grow some potatoes, because you're going to want fries with that. After a long season of hard work, you'll have your cheeseburger, and it'll be the freshest, most rewarding meal you ever had. But what if you've never raised cattle before? What do they eat? How much space do they need? Why is that big one staring at you like that?

With home buying, there are so many steps and so many people involved that things can get pretty hairy. And, unfortunately, it's easy to run into someone who will be all too willing to take advantage of you. The entire purchasing process would be so much easier if you had some idea of what to expect, how to deal with it, and where to find help—from a source that isn't so complicated that you wish you'd just opened a cattle ranch instead.

That's where this book comes in.

Why Am I Writing This?

Why? Because I wish I had known before buying my first house what I know now as I sit comfortably in my fifth. No, I'm not a mortgage expert, real estate agent, or financial advisor. What I am is a consumer—just like you. A consumer who has bought five houses (so far) and sold four (so far). I bought my first house to stop renting and start building my personal American dream. The next three came from job transfers. The most recent gives me less to vacuum and no more snow to shovel (thankfully), except to dig out my car when the plow traps it in. I confess. I am a serial homeowner. And more than once, I've been in your shoes (nice shoes!).

With my first home buying experience, I had more than my share of surprises. I discovered that buying a house, especially the first time, can be quite an emotional experience. It's surprisingly easy to get attached to one house or another. And because I was not as organized or knowledgeable as I needed to be, I made many emotional decisions. When you make decisions with your emotions, it becomes all too easy to overlook potential problems with the property because you've fallen in love with an extra room in the basement or something shiny in the kitchen. You can end up with mortgage payments that are too high, hefty repair bills, or other costs that wreak havoc on your checkbook—all because your heart says you must, *must*, have *this* house with *that* thing in it.

Of course, a big part of any house hunt involves discovering a house that "feels" right. But those feelings can sometimes run rings around sound financial decisions. While home ownership *is* about the right number of rooms or the size of the garage, it's also about protecting your financial future. So as you look for a place that will make you happy, you'll need to think of and treat your purchase as a business transaction. That means getting organized, gathering information, making preparations, and finding the help you need to land those keys in your hand.

My purpose is to contribute to the knowledge you need to navigate your way through a seemingly endless series of critical decisions. How? By helping you understand the basics.

What's In This Book?

The following chapters will give you a glimpse of the entire home buying process: the financial preparation, loan, house hunt, contract, sale, and settling in. The book is divided into three sections: a preparation phase, a house hunting phase, and a contract and buying phase. Each step of the way, I'll describe the process and share a few of my own and others' experiences, mistakes and all.

You'll read about some of the more common things buyers encounter, things to consider, questions to ask, and sources of helpful information. Many of the terms you'll run into as you navigate the path to home ownership will be defined. You may find that you already know some of them, but I don't assume. The definitions are there if you need them.

I've also enlisted the help of several experts—real estate agents, mortgage loan officers, a settlement agent, financial and tax consultants, a title agent, and home inspection and insurance professionals—to introduce you to the types of people you'll be working with and to add a professional point of view. Finally, in the Appendix, there are a few charts to help you organize your thoughts. When you see *"Chart Attack!"* in the chapters, you'll know it's time to flip to the Appendix to fill in a few blanks.

The intent of this book isn't to include every possible situation you may face, nor is it to tell you what decisions are best for you. Everyone's needs are unique, and no two houses or transactions are the same. Remember, I'm a consumer like you, not an expert. Always consult the professionals for advice on your specific situation. If you read the second paragraph on the Copyright page, you get the idea.

By the way, to keep things neat and tidy, I use the word "house" as a generic term for whatever you end up living in. It can be a traditional single family house, a townhouse, a condominium, or a grass hut on a hillside, but I'll call it a "house" regardless. It's so much easier this way.

Who Will Benefit From This Book?

This is a book for both first-time and other buyers who want to understand and organize the overall buying process better. It's geared toward those who are buying one house in the United States as a primary residence (not for vacation, investment, or rental property). It's a book for people who want the process described in plain English.

ON YOUR MARK...
GET SET... PREPARE!

The very first time the house buying bug bit me, I jumped right in. I called a real estate agent and hit the road the next day on a hunt for the "perfect" house. After all, I had figured out how to get some down payment money together. I had asked my homeowner friends and relatives about what they had done and heard the stories of their experiences. I had looked at listings in the paper and a few other places. Surely, these were preparations enough, right?

No.

While the steps I took were a good start, I could have saved myself a lot of time and anxiety if I had had a better plan of attack, especially when it came to my financial realities and how buying a house would affect them. You see, before you buy, you need to have a good handle on your finances so you'll have realistic expectations about what you can and cannot afford. Then you can make realistic decisions about what home to buy and protect yourself from those who wouldn't mind taking your money and leaving you with something that's not right for you.

In this section, you'll learn to:
- Put together a team of professionals
- Review your credit and finances
- Familiarize yourself with home loans
- Apply for a loan

2

THE "I" (OR "WE") IN TEAM

A re you ready to take the plunge? Yes? Well, then, you need to plan. As I mentioned earlier, buying a house can be a very emotional experience. But however you're *feeling*, you need to *think* business. So put on your businessperson hat. If you were the president of a brand new company, you'd gather the information and resources you already had and figure out what else you'd need to make things happen. Then you'd surround yourself with capable experts—your team—and delegate responsibilities accordingly. Well, your company's goal is to buy the right house for you, so choose your team wisely.

Who Are All These People?

As company president, your job is to hire a team that will help you get what you want: the right house at the lowest possible price, a mortgage with the most favorable terms you can get, a house that's compatible with your financial and personal needs, and an uneventful, low-stress purchase.

Throughout this book, you'll learn about the following professionals and their roles in your journey to ownership:

- a *mortgage lender* (the company) and *mortgage loan officer* (the person you'll work with) to help you get the money you need

- a *real estate agent* to help you find that new place

- a *financial advisor* to help make your purchase fit within your financial goals

- a *builder* if you're venturing into new construction territory

- an *attorney* to help you wade through the contract and sale (more common in some states than in others)

- a *home inspector* to find hidden (or not so hidden) flaws before you buy

- a *title company* and *title agent* to transfer the property from the seller to you

- an *insurance agent* to provide the coverage you'll need

- a *mover* to save wear and tear on your back

Can you believe how many people it can take to buy one little house? This list includes almost anyone that may be included in your home purchase. Which people you'll actually need will depend on your situation and how much work or risk you're willing to take on. Sound expensive? Some of their fees are paid on the day you buy your house. Some are a matter of paying a little money now to save a lot of money, time, headaches, risk—or whatever else is important to you—later.

Corporate Relocations. If your employer is moving you and you're eligible for relocation benefits, your relocation specialist or human resources representative will also be a valuable member of your team. Get to know the relocation policy. Learn what your employer will do and pay for and what you'll have to cover on your own.

You're in Charge

Every president wants to surround him- or herself with the best talent. So should you. There's not a profession in the world that doesn't have its good and bad. To find the right team for your home purchase, you'll need to do more than choose the first name you see in the phone book, so give yourself time to make the right choice. Fortunately you don't have to choose them all at once. You'll need a real estate agent long before you'll need a settlement company, for example.

I'll have more to say about choosing each professional in the chapters ahead. But often your best bet is to ask relatives, friends, and colleagues who have been through the process. If they had a good experience with a professional, they won't hesitate to recommend him or her. If you're eligible for your employer's relocation benefits, you may receive a list of people. Also, once you've identified one professional, he or she often can recommend others.

Your team, if you choose well, will provide timely information, make recommendations that benefit you, warn you about risks, steer you in the right direction, and teach you about the process. But the final decisions are yours. Remember, you're the one who will have to live with the results—both the house and the finances—for a long time. And unless they're going to live with you, your home buying experience will never mean the same to your team members as it will to you.

So if you don't like a particular neighborhood, you're not comfortable with the terms of a loan, you don't understand the fine print, or your great-grandmother's china is getting jostled around too much, speak up! Explain your concerns and make sure they're addressed to your satisfaction. It's your money, your stuff, your home, your life. And they're your team.

3.

WHERE CREDIT IS DUE

I 'm going to assume that you, like most people, do not have a lot of cash stuffed inside a lumpy mattress. So you'll need a rather sizable home loan—a *mortgage*—to cover most of the cost. But before you even think of applying for that mortgage, make sure your finances are presentable. Are they in good shape? How are your spending habits? Have you consistently paid your bills on time? Do you stick to a budget?

The first thing you can do to assess the state of your financial health is to take a look at the same document the mortgage lenders will look at: your *credit report*—a history of how you've handled your loans and credit cards. This report, the gossip column of your personal finances, shamelessly tells all your business!

Jason Werther, loan officer, says that your report will include loans, mortgages, credit cards, any bills that were referred to collection agencies, bankruptcies, and any other debts you've taken on in the past several years. It also includes any inquiries from new creditors (such as credit card companies when you apply for a new card) about your creditworthiness. Your rental history will not appear on your report.

Credit Reporting Agencies

There are three major credit reporting agencies, and you can get reports from them once per year or any time you're denied credit. It's a good idea to get copies of all three reports, since they may contain different information.

Equifax
800-685-1111
www.equifax.com

Experian
National Consumer Assistance Center
888-EXPERIAN (888-397-3742)
www.experian.com/consumer

Trans Union
Consumer Disclosure Center
800-888-4213
www.transunion.com

Get your credit report as early in the home buying process as possible. If anything needs your attention, you'll need time to work on it.

How'd You Do on Your Report Card?

When you get your report, first make sure that everything is accurate. Mistakes can happen. I once found that a credit card I had canceled years earlier still appeared on my report as active. I gave the creditor and the agency the information they needed to report the credit card information accurately. It took a while, but they corrected it.

If you find a mistake, contact the credit reporting agency and the creditor. They'll ask for any documentation you have to support your claim. Start early; it can take at least a month or two to get mistakes corrected, Kevin Mahoney, loan officer, says. If you're hoping to buy your house in less than thirty to sixty days, ask a financial advisor if he or she can help you move things along.

Next look at your *credit score*. Scores are usually between 300 and 800 (which may give you flashbacks of the SAT), though they can be higher. Theoretically, the higher the score, the more likely you are to repay your debts on time. You'll have a score from each of the three credit agencies, and chances are they'll all be different. Yeah. Go figure.

Mortgage lenders, Jason Werther says, often use the middle score for your application, and they usually prefer a minimum score of about 620. In some areas and for some loans, Kevin Mahoney says, that minimum can be higher. If your score is below the minimum, it doesn't necessarily mean you're out of the running. But it does mean you may need to find a lender that works with clients with lower scores. You may have to work harder to get the loan you need.

Stumbling Blocks

Blemishes on your credit report lower your credit score. By "blemishes" I mean things that make mortgage lenders less willing to fork over that large sum of money you'll need. Here are a few:

- making late payments on your debts
- missing payments on your debts
- declaring bankruptcy
- having a collection agency chase after you
- maintaining high credit card balances compared to your limits
- applying for a lot of new credit card accounts

Art Auerbach, Certified Public Accountant (CPA), says that having lots of high-limit credit cards, even if you're not using them, can sometimes raise issues, too. Why? Because you could lose your mind one afternoon and shop yourself silly, right on up to the limits. You'd never do that? Well, the point is that you could. A financial advisor can help you figure out whether this is an issue for you, and if it is, what you should do about it.

Do any of those "blemishes" listed above sound familiar? If so, the credit reporting agencies know all about it. Any problem you have will be on your credit report, jumping out and waving its hands like it's proud of itself. Is that problem on your record a one-time thing or a recurring event? Was there one problem or were there many? Whatever the case, you can't hide, you can't run, so just be prepared to explain it all. The rest will be up to the lender.

Will this hurt your chances at a mortgage? Possibly. It can mean anything from getting less favorable terms from your mortgage lender—maybe less money or a higher interest rate—or not being approved at all. But there are ways to improve your credit and therefore your chances. For example, you can lower your credit card and loan balances and establish a history of paying your bills on time. If you're not sure what to do, turn to a financial advisor to help you work out a plan to improve your credit rating and your overall financial health. Improving your credit is one of the most important steps you can take to assure you're home buying experience goes smoothly.

No Credit Record?

What if you've never had any credit cards or loans? Or you're using credit cards, but they're not in your own name? A mortgage lender won't have any proof that you can handle a loan. So you'll need to *establish credit*—create a credit history for yourself.

Knowing and Understanding Your Credit, a publication by the Fannie Mae Foundation and the National Endowment for Financial Education, suggests compiling a "nontraditional history." This is "your own report to show a lender that you pay your rent, telephone, car insurance, medical, and utility bills on time each month."[1] To build a report, you can pull together recent bills and request letters from your landlord and other creditors.

Also, if you use credit cards or other services that are in your spouse's or someone else's name, they won't appear on your own credit report, no matter how responsibly you handle them. You'll need some accounts in your own name for that.[2]

Beware of Identity Theft

These days identity theft is always a threat. If there are things on your report you don't recognize, or the report otherwise looks strange and you suspect identity theft, contact the reporting agency immediately. Asserting the fraudulent use of your name and personal information can get messy and may take a while to clean up. You may need legal help. If so, don't just roam through the phone book. Make sure you find a legal professional who is

---

What's in Print?
For a free copy of *Knowing and Understanding Your Credit,* published by the Fannie Mae Foundation and the National Endowment for Financial Education:
- Direct link: www.homebuyingguide.org
- Also: www.fanniemaefoundation.org, click "Publications," click "Home-Buying Guides"
- Phone: 1-800-611-9566

experienced in dealing with these issues. Because of the serious issues involved in erasing the stain of identity theft, you may want to consider putting off the mortgage application until your record has been corrected.

4

FINANCES: A PLAN FOR ALL SEASONS

When you're preparing to buy a home, it's important to take a good look at your finances. In addition to the credit issues I just described, you will have to figure out how much house you can afford and how much money you can come up with up front. But don't stop there. Look at your whole financial picture. Buying a house will change that picture, and you'll also need to understand how your purchase will affect you, financially, in the long run.

A Wiser Advisor

Home buying time is a great time to get together with a financial advisor to help you wade through all these money matters. If you don't already have a financial advisor, ask people you trust for recommendations. Look for one who works with people in your income range and who can understand your specific needs—which now include a house. Your financial advisor will be someone who will have a hand in moving your hard earned money around, so don't rely solely on a little bit of information in an ad. Ask questions of any potential advisors and the people who recommend them. Talk about what you need and what they can do for you. Then choose carefully.

Your Financial Plan

If you're renting right now, your home is simply a monthly expense. But once you buy, you'll have an *asset*—something of financial value to you. This value is *equity*—the current market value of your house minus your mortgage and any other debts attached to your purchase. A colleague of mine bought a house in 1955 for under $23,000. In 1974 that same house was worth about $175,000, and by 2000 the value was hovering around $600,000. Talk about equity!

You can increase your equity by paying your mortgage and making certain improvements to the house. Equity can also increase thanks to things completely out of your control, such as favorable market conditions or improvements to the surrounding area. Naturally, if equity can increase, it can also decrease. Neglecting the house's maintenance needs, an unfavorable market, and deteriorating conditions in the areas are a few things that can make your equity drop. No one can guarantee that your house will increase in value like my colleague's did, but you can better your chances with careful planning and decision making. Plan to protect your investment.

Sue van der Linden, financial advisor, says it's important to work the asset your home becomes into your new financial picture. For example, what will this house be to you, primarily? A home for your family for generations? An investment you'll live in for a while? How long do you think you'll want to keep it? And although we don't like to think of such things, what will happen to your house if you die or become incapacitated?

Your purchase, your asset, needs to blend in with your other plans. Maybe your kids will be starting college in ten years. Maybe you're concerned about retirement. Maybe you just want to save some money. Questions and considerations such as these will help you decide what kind of house and mortgage are right for you.

Who Needs a Plan? Financial planning isn't just for people in high tax brackets with excess money to invest. It's for all people who have responsibility for the money they bring home and live on. Your needs may not be as elaborate as those of the millionaire across town, but if you can qualify for a mortgage, certainly you have enough income to make a plan. And now you'll have an asset to look after. If you're not sure how to go about developing a plan, take yourself on down to a financial advisor's office, sharpen your pencil, and have at it.

Taxes

Buying a house has a big effect on your taxes. If you've been renting and you're buying for the first time, that old 1040EZ might not fit the bill anymore. When you file your tax return that next year, you'll find things have gotten a little more...involved. Your house will become another thing, along with your income, marital status, number of dependents, and so on, that will influence your tax calculations. According to CPA Art Auerbach, mortgage interest (in part or in full) and real estate taxes are deductible expenses on your federal and state tax returns.

Exemptions. Art suggests looking at the exemptions you list with your employer for payroll deduction purposes. You remember that form: it asks you to lists your dependents, including yourself, add them up and turn in that magic number so the people who cut the checks know how much of your paycheck goes to taxes. Adjusting your exemptions means more or less money comes out of your salary. Ask your financial advisor whether you should adjust your exemptions—change the amount you get in take-home pay versus the amount you pay or get refunded when you file—to reflect your new tax situation.

Tax Credits. A number of states, financial advisor Sue van der Linden says, offer a *tax credit*—a reduction in the taxes you owe— for some first-time home buyers. For more information, contact your state tax department or check that department's website.

Corporate Relocations. If you're eligible for your employer's corporate relocation program, some of those benefits may be considered taxable income. Ask your employer and financial advisor about the details and the best way for you to handle them. Some people find that it's in their financial interest not to accept certain relocation benefits. You'll need the help of a financial advisor to determine whether that applies to you.

Your Monthly House Bill...

As a part of your assessment of your overall financial picture, it's time to turn to your monthly situation. Given the money you currently bring in, how much can you afford to pay per month for housing? Take a look at your current monthly household income, debts, and other expenses. Are you comfortable with your current rent or mortgage payment? Can you afford more and still have enough for your other expenses and financial goals? Would you rather pay less?

As a rule of thumb, mortgage lenders typically target about 36% of total income for debt payments (such as loans and credit cards). That includes housing. For housing alone, the rule of thumb is 28% of income. Based on your current income, is your housing payment hovering anywhere near those figures? Understand, though, that the actual percentages a mortgage lender might apply to you may be higher or lower than the 36% and 28% depending on the shape of your finances (more on this in Chapter 6).

So what's the maximum monthly housing payment you can handle? Consider "buying what you're comfortable making the payments on now, not what you think you can afford later," financial advisor Sue van der Linden says. Otherwise it might be more difficult than you think to catch up if your income doesn't increase the way you anticipated.

This is a critical point. You don't want to be in a position where you *default* on—fail to pay—your mortgage payments. It's not like missing a rent payment. While that isn't a happy situation, it won't have the same impact as failing to pay for your house. Missing mortgage payments affects your credit record and your ability to get another loan in the future. You can even lose your house. So if you're going to buy it, you have to be able to pay for it without fail.

...And Your Other House Bills

If you're buying for the first time, you'll need to work a few additional things into your budget. Once you're a homeowner, you can't call the landlord anymore, because, well, that's you! CPA Art Auerbach says, "When you buy a house, you buy another dependent." I can tell you from experience, it sure feels that way. Your new dependent may not spit out its food when you want it to eat or run away laughing when you're trying to get it dressed (if it does, you should reconsider your investment!), but it will most definitely complain *expensively* if you ignore it when it cries. So be financially prepared to budget for your mortgage, plus:

Homeowners Association or Condominium Fee. If you buy a condominium or townhouse, some things on the outside of the house will be handled by a homeowner's association, and you'll pay a monthly fee (covered in Chapter 9). In some cases, this can also apply to single family homes. These fees can increase from time to time, often annually. Also, Art says, they are generally not tax deductible.

Utilities. The amount you pay for utilities will depend, in part, on the area you'll live in. And the bigger the house, the more space there is to heat and cool. If some utilities were included in your rent, you'll have to get used to paying for them separately. If you pay a homeowners association or condominium fee, you'll need to know if it includes any utilities.

Repairs and Emergencies. If a tree falls in the forest, it might not make a sound. If it falls on your house, *you* certainly will! An air conditioner that breaks down in July or a water pipe that freezes and bursts in January will need your attention—*fast.* Your budget has to include some plan for making sure you have the funds to deal with unexpected emergencies. CPA Art Auerbach says, for example, that you can put six to eight months worth of expenses in a certificate of deposit (CD) or money market account for emergencies.

Maintenance and Improvements. Maintenance usually costs a lot less than repairs, so it's worth your time and money to keep things in good shape. And if you like home improvement projects, your new home guarantees there will always be something that can use your special touch (or the touch of someone you hire). Be prepared to work these expenses into your plans. And if you do decide to make improvements, keep in mind that some projects require permits, inspections, and compliance with building codes.

chartattack!

Use **Charts A and B** in the Appendix to calculate your monthly income and budget.

Money You Need Up Front

How much cash do you have available right now to put toward a new house? While your mortgage will be the primary source of financing for your new house, it usually won't cover the full cost of the house and won't include other expenses associated with the purchase. There are some expenses you'll need to take care of before or on the day you buy. To cover those expenses plus a down payment, you'll need cash.

Without yet knowing how much mortgage you'll qualify for or what house you'll buy, just work for now on getting an idea of the maximum amount you can come up with. Who knows, you might not need the full amount. But with this figure in mind, you'll know what does and does not fit your financial plan as you go through the buying process. Things you'll need to cover include:

The Down Payment. This is the difference between your mortgage and the purchase price of the house, and you pay it on the day of the purchase. It can be a sticking point for a lot of potential home owners. They would buy a home in a heartbeat if only they could come up with that dreaded down payment.

Some mortgages require a minimum down payment, such as 10% or 20% of the house's purchase price. Others, especially some mortgage programs designed for first-time buyers, require smaller down payment amounts, such as 5% of the purchase price or none at all. How much you will need depends on what you can work out with your lender. And how much cash you put down can determine whether you'll be required to pay *private mortgage insurance (PMI)*—an insurance that protects the lender's investment (covered in Chapter 5).

Closing Costs. These are costs paid on your *settlement date*—the day you buy your house—and are additional costs associated with the buying process, such as lender fees, insurance premiums, and other fees (covered in Chapter 13).

Deposit. When you make an offer on a house, you'll be asked to provide a *deposit* (or *earnest money*) that will be held until the settlement date (covered in Chapter 10). The deposit is applied to the purchase price.

Home Inspection. Before you finalize your offer to buy a house, you will have the option of requesting a home inspection, where a professional inspector checks the house from top to bottom for any potential problems (covered in Chapter 11). The fee for a home inspection is usually paid at the time of inspection.

Moving Expenses. Whether you hire a moving company or do it yourself, you'll have to spend some money here, too (covered in Chapter 12).

Appraisal Fee. The lender will hire a professional appraiser to assess the value of the property you're buying. The appraiser's fee will either be paid before the appraisal or as part of closing costs when you buy.

And Where is All This Money Supposed to Come From, Hmm?

Sounds like there's a lot of money involved, right? There is. But there are also several ways to pull it all together, such as:

Savings. The first source of cash, of course, is your savings account. If you started saving early and diligently, your savings account might be all you'll need.

chartattack!
Use **Chart C** in the Appendix to fill in your up-front money needed as the information becomes available.

Retirement Accounts. According to financial advisor Sue van der Linden, you can withdraw up to $10,000 from your IRA without penalty *once in your lifetime* if you use it specifically to buy a house *and* you've made contributions of at least $2,000 per year in the previous five years. Taxes will still apply for a conventional IRA. If you have a Roth IRA, CPA Art Auerbach says, special rules will apply to a withdrawal. Ask your retirement plan administrator for details. Plan carefully before taking anything from these accounts, however. You're not only losing the money you took out, but the future money it could have earned. If you withdraw money from a retirement account, make sure it's consistent with your overall financial plans.

If you participate in your employer's 401k savings plan, you can borrow money from your account. Sue van der Linden says that if you're requesting the money specifically for the purchase of a house, you can take anywhere from five to 30 years to make payments on that loan. The specific time allowed depends on the plan. Check with your employer and make sure you know the rules, the pros, and the cons before you sign on.

Again, be sure borrowing against your 401k is in keeping with your overall financial plans, and understand that a mortgage lender will see this loan as additional debt (more on debt and mortgages in Chapter 6). True, it's a loan but at least you're paying yourself back—not another creditor. How often does that happen? By the way, Art Auerbach suggests that you check with your financial advisor to find out whether the interest you're paying yourself is tax deductible.

Rules and laws governing these plans can change from time to time, so familiarize yourself with those that apply at the time you decide to touch your accounts. And one final point. Give yourself time to get a loan or withdrawal processed. It can take several weeks from the time you apply until you get a check in your hands, so don't wait until a few days before you need it to ask for it.

chartattack!

Use **Chart D** in the Appendix to help you calculate the most cash you can come up with from the different sources at your disposal. Start with the resources you're aware of now, and fill in the blanks as additional information becomes available.

Sale of Your Current House. If you already own a house and you're selling it to buy the new one, the money you make from that sale can go toward your down payment… that is, if the sale makes a profit. If the sale only covers the obligations of your current mortgage or is for less than your current mortgage, you won't have those funds available to apply to your new purchase.

Gift. Some buyers, especially first timers, receive a gift (*not* a loan) from relatives to help them with the purchase of their house. The gift is verified through a *gift letter*, a signed letter from the gift giver, stating that the money was given for the purchase of a house and that you aren't expected to pay the money back. Your lender may have a form available for this. Family and money don't always mix well, so ask yourself if asking for a gift will cause any problems before you go for it. No need to end up on the "family feud" episode of a daytime talk show.

Loan. It is possible to borrow down payment money. Again, that will count as debt and can affect your mortgage application. Unless you have very little debt from other sources, borrowing money for a down payment just might defeat the purpose.

5.

DIAL "M" FOR MORTGAGE

So now you've decided how much cash you have available for your purchase and the maximum monthly payment you're willing to take on. You know what shape your credit is in, and if needed, you've done what you can to correct or improve it. Congratulations! You're ready to find a mortgage.

Applying for a mortgage can be one of the more intimidating parts of the entire home buying process. When I bought House #1, I was a few years out of school. I had a paycheck, a modest budget, the usual bills, and a few investments with my employer's savings plan. At that point in my life, my biggest financial transaction had been a little blue hatchback that I truly wished had power windows.

Now here I was with this mortgage lender, talking in sums larger than I'd ever dealt with before and asking me to send them everything but my heart and lungs as proof of my trustworthiness. Enough paper passed between them and me to fuel the Great Chicago Fire. But in the end they decided to take a chance on me, and my era of serial homeownership began.

Wondering why I put this section before the actual house hunt? After all, how do you know how much you'll need if you

---

don't yet know what you want to buy? Well, if you go to a real estate agent (and you can do that first, if you prefer; many people do), one of the first things he or she will ask you for is a price range. Your agent won't want to show you $350,000 houses if your limit turns out to be $200,000. You won't be able to answer that question if you haven't started the mortgage process. Most agents will recommend you get mortgage approval before you start looking at houses.

In the mortgage application process, a mortgage lender will tell you the maximum amount the company is willing to give you toward the purchase of your house, regardless of what you want to buy. Add the mortgage lender's maximum to your down payment money, and you'll know the highest priced house you can afford. And you won't waste time looking at and falling in love with a house that's too expensive. You might even find something for less than your maximum mortgage loan and not need the entire amount. But you'll know your limits, and your real estate agent will know what to target for you. Here's what you're aiming for at this point:

Pre-Qualification. Getting pre-qualified is the process I just described. It means that you've applied for a mortgage, and without yet knowing what house you will buy, your lender has determined the maximum amount they will lend you. This is different from:

Pre-Approval. Once you've found the house you want, your loan officer will give you a letter stating the purchase price, your down payment and loan details, and information about the specific house you want to buy, Jean Keller, loan officer, says. This letter will be good for somewhere between 30 and 60 days. If you don't buy your house before then, the loan officer will need to run your credit again and issue a new letter.

Anatomy of a Mortgage

What does a mortgage look like? Three primary factors make up the loan—the type of loan, the *interest rate*, and the *loan period*. These form a sum consisting of two elements—*principal* and *interest.* Added to this amount are *taxes* and *insurance.* Once you buy your house, you'll have *monthly payments*, consisting of all four elements, that will rifle through your checkbook like just your rent used to. But this time at least you're paying for your own property, not someone else's!

Let's start by defining those four elements that will show up on your statement every month.

- *Principal.* The actual amount of money you borrow.

- *Interest.* The amount you pay for the use of that money.

- *Taxes.* Property taxes determined by your local authorities.

- *Insurance. Homeowner's insurance*, provided by your insurance carrier, and sometimes *private mortgage insurance (PMI).*

You'll often see a couple of acronyms associated with these:

- *PITI.* Principal, Interest, Taxes, and Insurance (Fitting acronym, isn't it, given the word it sort of spells out?)

- *P+I.* Principal and Interest only. These two terms are sometimes set apart because taxes and insurance are determined separately.

Escrow. When you set up PITI payments, your lender will hold the tax and insurance portions of your monthly payment in *escrow*—in a non-interest bearing account. When billed by tax authorities or insurance company, the lender pays the bills from that account.

If you prefer to pay taxes and insurance yourself, you can ask your loan officer to arrange for P+I only. That means you'll receive and pay property insurance, homeowner's insurance and any other tax or insurance bills directly. You'll get to keep and earn interest on your money a little longer, but paying these bills directly will mean more bills to keep up with every month, quarter, or year. Be aware, though, that some loans place restrictions on allowing the homeowner to pay these bills directly, loan officer Kevin Mahoney adds. Ask your loan officer about it.

Amortization. One other thing to be aware of: Interest will represent a bigger chunk of your P+I in the earlier years of the loan. With each payment, this gradually changes so that in the latter years, your payment is mostly principal. This is called *amortization*.

Let's say the terms of a loan give you a monthly P+I of $1,200. In the example below, look what happens to the principal and interest throughout the life of the loan. Just to keep things nice and neat, I used 10% and 90% of the total for principal and interest toward the beginning and end of the loan.

	Earlier Payment	Somewhere in the Middle	Later Payment
Principal	$ 120	$ 600	$1,080
Interest	$1,080	$ 600	$ 120
Total P+I	$1,200	$1,200	$1,200

Why does this happen? So that lenders can make their money (interest) in the earlier years of your loan. If you default half way through your loan, they've already made most of their money. Is this unusual? No. You'll find that a lot of loans work the same way. If you want to know exactly how this will break down for your own loan, Jason Werther suggests asking your loan officer for an *amortization chart*.

The Principal of the Thing

The *principal* is simply the amount of money you're going to borrow and use to pay for your house. The amount available to you will depend on the shape of your credit and your ability to make payments. When you're ready to buy your house, your lender will wire that money to your *title company*—the company that handles the final transaction (covered in Chapter 13)—to fund your purchase.

Something of Interest

As with any loan, a mortgage *interest rate* is a percentage of the principal and determines how much you'll have to pay your lender for the use of their money. Mortgage rates show up in one-eighth increments, so you'll see rates with as many as three decimal places, such as 7.125%, 6%, 8.25%, 6.375, or 5.5%. In ads, lower rates may be accompanied by bright colors and at least one exclamation point.

Because of the interest rate's effect on both the principal you can qualify for and your monthly payment, the interest rate alone can make the difference between getting the house you really want and having to settle for one for a lower price, or between buying a house at all and having to wait. Here's an example from loan officer Jean Keller:

You get a $200,000 loan with an interest rate of 6.5%. With the other terms of the loan, it has a monthly payment within your budget. But what if that same loan had an interest rate of 8.25%?

Interest Rate	Monthly P+I
6.50%	$1,265
8.25%	$1,500

That's a difference of $2,820 a year. And don't forget you'll also have taxes and insurance added to that. Let's say that's $235 per month:

Interest Rate	Monthly P+I	Monthly T+I	Monthly PITI
6.50%	$1,265	$235	$1,500
8.25%	$1,500	$235	$1,735

Quite a difference, isn't it? Let's take the example a bit further. What if, when assessing your finances, you decided that the maximum monthly payment you can afford is $1,600, but you only qualified for the 8.25% interest rate above? That's over your budget. Then what? There are a few things you can discuss with your loan officer:

- Try to qualify for a different type of loan with the same principal.

- Accept a lower principal and increase your down payment.

- Accept a lower principal, keep your current down payment, and buy a less expensive house.

Locking In. When you're approved for a loan, your interest rate isn't set until you *lock in*—set your rate at the rate that applies at that moment. Interest rates can fluctuate with changes in the real estate market—sometimes several times a day. Your rate will float right along with the market until it's locked in.

You can do this immediately, or you can let it float for days or weeks. Why let it float? Because sometimes rates can decrease. Of course, they can increase just as easily. There's no guarantee which way they'll go, and your loan officer has no control over it.

Lock-in periods are generally good for 30 to 60 days, so if you don't buy your house by then, you'll have to lock in again. And your rate may change. So talk it over with your loan officer, then, as loan officer Jean Keller says, request a *lock-in commitment* to officially lock in your rate when you think it's best. When it's done, loan officer Jason Werther suggests asking for a *lock-in confirmation*—a letter or e-mail stating your final interest rate—so there are no misunderstandings later in the process.

Basic Loan Types...

While there are several types of mortgages available, most fall into one of two broad categories—*fixed* and *adjustable*.

Fixed Rate Mortgage. Your interest rate will be established at the time your loan is approved and will remain the same for the life of your loan. In this case, your monthly P+I will not change. For example, a 30-year fixed rate loan will have the same P+I for each of your 360 monthly payments. The advantage of this kind of loan is that you'll always know how much P+I you need to pay every month. The only things that can change are the taxes and insurance portions of your payment.

Adjustable Rate Mortgage (ARM). This type is more complicated. An initial interest rate will be established at the time your loan is approved, then that rate will change at specified intervals— *adjustment periods*. This can be every year or every several years (commonly three, five, or seven). For example, if you select a five-year period, your interest rate will remain stable for five years then adjusts up or down each adjustment period depending on the state of the market, economy, and terms of your loan at the time of the adjustment. These loans tend to have lower initial interest rates than fixed-rate loans, because you're taking on more risk.

When you get an ARM, you'll have no idea what your interest rate will be after that initial period. Your new monthly payment will increase or decrease depending on the change in interest rates, so this can have a significant effect on your checkbook. Here's an example from loan officer Jason Werther, showing what can happen when interest rates increase over time. In this example, the initial rate yields a monthly P+I payment of $1,000. Here's how the P+I payment can change when rates increase.

Adjustment Period	Interest Rate	Monthly Payment	Annual Increase Over Original Payment
Initial	6%	$1,000	
1	8%	$1,224	$2,688
2	10%	$1,464	$5,568

When considering an ARM, you have to decide how much risk you can tolerate. Can you handle potentially significant increases five, ten, or fifteen years from now? Do you plan to keep the house that long? Loan officer Jean Keller says that if you know you'll own the house for less than five to seven years, for example, an ARM may work well, because you won't reach the first adjustment period. Give your situation plenty of thought and ask plenty of questions before taking on the risk.

To help protect you, adjustable rate loans typically include a limit—*cap*—on the amount of increase in your interest rate. If, for example, your loan has a 2% cap, your rate cannot increase by more than 2 percentage points over your previous rate, even if the prevailing rate increase is higher. Just remember that if, for example, your rate increases by 2 percentage points every five years, an initial 6% rate can become 10% in ten years if prevailing rates happen to reach that high. You'll have to be prepared to pay those extra dollars. Ask the loan officer to explain how a rate cap would work for your loan should interest rates increase or decrease over the life of the loan.

If your loan has a **payment cap**—a cap on the *monthly payment* increase (not on the interest rate) as a percentage of the previous monthly payment—it's possible to have a situation where your monthly payment, with cap, doesn't cover all of the interest.[3] This will add to your debt and actually increase the amount you owe your lender. This, Jean Keller says, is known as **negative amortization**. Ask your loan officer about this possibility if you are considering an ARM with a payment cap.

...And Special Loan Types

There are other types of loans that have special features or are designed for people with special circumstances.

Balloon/Reset Mortgages. This is an adjustable mortgage with a rather dramatic twist. Your P+I is set for a defined number of years, such as five or seven. As soon as that period is over—when you reach the *maturity date* of the loan—*you will owe the remaining principal. All at once.* Thus the name "balloon." Yup. *Pop!*

Loan officer Jason Werther says that this can be a good choice if you plan to sell the house before the maturity date, because of the relatively lower interest rate. Beyond the maturity date, you have the option to convert, or **reset** your loan to a 30-year fixed mortgage at the interest rates available at the time of the reset. But certain conditions may have to be met before the reset is allowed. Talk to the loan officer about that.

Interest-Only Loans. For the first several years of these fixed or adjustable loans, you pay only the interest and no principal. So instead of PITI, you just get ITI. This means lower monthly payments for a few years, and maybe the ability to buy a house you wouldn't have been able to afford with other types of loans. But because you pay no principal, you build no equity in your house during the first few years. With some of these loans, you can add principal on top of the required interest with your monthly payment. Someone with variable income, for example, might do this if the commission is especially good that month.

Later, you start paying both principal and interest for the rest of the life of the loan. This means significantly higher monthly payments because first, you're now required to pay principal on top of interest, and second, you now have fewer years left to pay the whole thing off. So as always, be sure to fully understand the details of an interest-only loan and its effect on your finances before taking one on.

Jumbo Loans. For those who need larger sums of money, these are fixed or adjustable rate loans above a specified minimum principal that changes from year to year. In 2005, this includes loans over $359,650.

Check with your loan officer for the current minimum if you think you'll need this kind of loan. The main difference with a jumbo loan, other than the dollar amount, is higher interest rates. Loans below the jumbo loan limit are called *conventional loans.*

Federal Housing Administration (FHA) Loans. These are for low- to moderate-income borrowers and those with lower credit scores who would otherwise have a hard time qualifying for a mortgage. These loans often require low down payments. These still come from a mortgage lender, but the federal government insures the loan to reduce the lender's risk.

Veterans Administration (VA) Loans. This federal program for veterans provides loans with low down payments. If you think you might qualify, you can get more information online or call the Veterans Administration Eligibility Center:

- www.homeloans.va.gov/veteran.htm
- 1-888-244-6711: if you live in the eastern half of the US
- 1-888-487-1970: if you live in the western half of the US

First-Time Buyer Programs. Some lenders have special fixed or adjustable rate mortgages designed to help the first-time buyer get over the hurdle of the down payment and other up-front costs. These programs are more risky for lenders, so a good credit score is especially important in order to qualify!

Will it Ever End?

The *loan period* (or *term*), is the number of years you'll be paying back your loan. Lenders typically offer loan periods of 10, 15, 20, and 30 years, though other periods are available. In general, the longer the loan period, the more interest you'll have paid by the time you've made your last payment. You're using their money longer, so you pay for that longer use with additional interest. On the other hand, with a shorter loan period, your monthly payment will be higher, because you're paying the principal back in less time. So consider the pros and cons when deciding whether you're better off with a higher monthly payment and less interest or a lower monthly payment and more interest in the long run. Think about the following questions:

- Do you think you'll be staying in the new house for several decades or just a few years?
- Is your income steady, or does it vary with things like bonuses and commissions?
- What best fits your overall financial plans?

Insurance

Homeowner's Insurance. When you get a mortgage, you'll be required to insure your home to protect your and your lender's investment (covered in Chapter 14). Homeowner's insurance covers your home in case of fire, disaster, or other unfortunate events.

Private Mortgage Insurance (PMI). To protect the lender from default, this additional insurance is mandatory if you buy your home with anything less than a 20% down payment. The cost of PMI varies with the price of the house. You'll pay a portion as a part of your *closing costs* (covered in Chapter 13), and the rest will be added to your monthly payment.

Notice that I said PMI protects the *lender.* Not you. You will continue to pay for PMI until you have paid enough principal to cover 20% of your house's purchase price. As you might recall from earlier in this chapter, in your first few years of loan payments, more of your money goes to interest than principal. If you've put down considerably less than a 20% down payment, you'll be paying PMI until you have added enough money to the "principal" column of your loan balance. That means you can be paying for PMI, money that will never contribute to your equity, for a good long time. And it's not tax deductible.

So if you don't want to pay PMI, what can you do? Here are a couple of options to talk to your loan officer and financial advisor about:

- Increase your down payment. If you have the resources to increase your down payment to at least 20%, you can avoid PMI altogether.

- Get a *second trust.* This is an additional loan that covers part of the down payment, thus giving you the whole 20%. Of course, this will also add to your debt.

One other thing you can consider is making additional payments on your principal along with your regular monthly payment. This won't get rid of PMI right away, but over time you'll reach the 20% mark faster. Be aware, though, that some loans may have restrictions on how much additional principal you can pay on your loan.

Loan Discount Points

Loan discount points, also called just *points*, are amounts you pay at settlement in exchange for better conditions of your loan, such as a lower interest rate. One point equals 1% of your loan amount. Is it worth it to pay this? Sometimes yes, sometimes no. Here's an example from loan officer Jason Werther.

You apply for a $200,000 loan.

A lender offers:	5.5% interest rate with 0 points
	5.125% interest rate with 1 point
1 point:	$2,000 (1% of $200,000)

If you choose to pay the $2,000 to get the lower interest rate, you save $47 in your monthly payment, and you make your $2,000 back in 43 months. With this information, you decide whether this benefits your financial goals.

What Else is In That Loan?

Loans come with additional fees. There are typically fees for processing the loan, paid at the time you buy your house. Other fees and requirements may be included as conditions of the loan, so always ask

chartattack!

If you've decided to pay points, add the amount to **Chart C** in the Appendix.

the loan officer to explain each one. Read all the documentation and ask questions if you don't understand.

A common fee with some loans is a ***prepayment penalty***. This is a fee you're charged if you pay off the loan *early*. Yes, you read that right. A penalty for paying early. Why on earth would a lender do such a thing? Because the sooner you pay your principal, the less interest you will owe, and the less the lender will make on the loan. Loan officer Kevin Mahoney says that prepayment penalties may stay in effect for the first several years of the loan and can also apply when you pay off the mortgage (and keep the house) or when you sell the house.

Some loans with penalty fees come with lower interest rates, lower points, or some other favorable feature in exchange for the risk. So first, ask enough questions to fully understand the terms of the loan. Think about your own plans. How long do you intend to own the house? How will this kind of loan fit with your finances? Then decide whether you can work with this fee included in your loan. If you can't, your best option is to seek another kind of loan.

6

THE PAPER CHASE: MORTGAGE APPLICATIONS

After familiarizing yourself with the basics of mortgages, it's time to start the actual application process. You'll be faced with a lot of options and paperwork, so patience will be a must. Be prepared to ask a lot of questions, answer even more, and read fine print. But the first step, of course, is to find a lender.

Anatomy of a Mortgage Lender

A quick glance through any newspaper or phone book will tell you that there are hundreds of lenders to choose from. So how do you find the right one for you? First, understand that there are three types of lenders:

Direct Mortgage Lenders. These companies specialize in mortgages and offer their own set of loans and services. They fund their loans, and all the behind-the-scenes processing is done in-house.

Mortgage Brokers. These are third parties that, on your behalf, shop for mortgages from among several lenders. Loan funding, processing, and customer service are handled by the actual lending organization.

Your Bank or Credit Union. In addition to its other services, your bank or credit union may also offer mortgages. They also fund and process their loans.

Assuming you qualify, any of these three types of lenders can provide a mortgage. The choice is about which fits your situation best.

Lenders, Lenders Everywhere

Choosing the right mortgage lender isn't necessarily the easiest thing you'll ever do. It seems like there are thousands out there, and some are even screaming at you through your television screen before you're properly awake for the day. How do you know which ones are reputable? And which one is right for you?

If you already have your real estate agent, he or she can point you in the direction of several trustworthy lenders. You can also ask friends, relatives, and coworkers to recommend a lender. There's no better recommendation than a happy customer. If your employer has a relocation department, ask people in that department for suggestions. Even if you're not eligible for relocation benefits, they might share with you a list of lenders.

Careful What You Wish For. While interest rates are important, don't just automatically choose a lender simply because it claims to have the lowest rate available or requires the smallest down payment. That seemingly amazing deal can come attached to some unpleasant conditions, like extra fees, and end up costing you more in the long run.

If you don't look into the lender's reputation, you can end up with a loan officer who's all but impossible to reach, monthly payments you truly can't afford, a pile of extra fees, or a loan that hasn't been processed in time for your settlement (meaning you won't be buying that house on Tuesday after all!). Your loan should have the right terms for your situation and the lowest interest rate you can *realistically* get. And your lender should provide reliable service.

In *Borrowing Basics: What You Don't Know Can Hurt You*, the Fannie Mae Foundation warns against **predatory lenders**. These lenders "offer loans based solely on the equity in a home, not on the borrower's ability to repay,...charge unusually high interest rates,... include excessive fees, and...tack on unnecessary costs, such as...life insurance."[4] To avoid predatory lending practices, stick with lenders you know or that are highly recommended by people you trust.

Service with a Smile. Don't neglect the lender's ability to provide customer service. Are they willing and able to answer lots of questions and respond quickly to a problem? When choosing a lender, look for one that will allow you to talk face to face or at least over the phone to an actual human being, who will personally become familiar with your case. Make sure you'll be able to deal with the same human being throughout the application process and settlement. Said human being should understand that because of the massive volume of personal information he or she will require of you, you may become temporarily overwhelmed and perhaps a bit discombobulated at some point in the process. Said human being should be patient and knowledgeable and should help you recover.

Big Brother Has a Microscope: The Application

When you apply for a mortgage, especially for the first time, be prepared to be scrutinized. Why? Because the mortgage company wants to know that giving you all that money is a safe thing to do. They want to know that you not only have the resources to pay them back, but that you'll actually do it.

For a 30-year loan, that's 360 payments, month after month, without fail. A lot can happen in 30 years. How do they know for sure that you'll pay them? Well, the only tool a mortgage lender has to predict the future is to look at how you've handled your money in the past. The lender will figure that if you've done well in paying your debts so far, you're more likely to continue to do so in the future. So here are some of the things they'll look at:

Your credit history. Have credit cards? Loans? How much do you owe? Are you running those credit cards up to the limit? Are you paying mortgages on any other properties? Have you ever filed for bankruptcy? Any late or missing bill payments? Has a creditor ever had to chase you down the street with a frying pan?

Your income. How much are you making in salary or wages, bonuses, and commissions? Do you get alimony, child support, rental income, investment income, any other form of cash that ultimately puts food on your table?

Your job. How long have you been working there? Have you been able to hold on to your jobs? Do you make enough to cover monthly payments in addition to your other obligations?

Your taxes. What's in this official record of your income and other money dealings? Any problems? Collections?

Although the exact documentation will vary slightly from one lender to the next, you should be prepared to give your lender at least the following information:

- Photo identification
- Your Social Security Number (they'll need this to get your credit report)
- Income documentation (pay stubs, bonuses, alimony or child support, etc.)
- Retirement savings
- Investments

- Bank statements (2 months)

- Tax returns or W-2 forms (2 years)

- Employment history (2 years)

- Residence history (2 years)

Other Documents. If you're already paying a mortgage, a history of your payments will appear on your credit report. If you've been renting, that history won't be there. But, loan officer Jean Keller says, the loan officer may contact your landlord to ensure that you paid your rent on time each month. He or she may also ask you for canceled checks as proof of rent payment, loan officer Kevin Mahoney adds, especially if your landlord is an individual rather than a property management company. In any case, lenders don't like to discover late payments. Not that landlords are happy campers over them, either.

The Finishing Touch

So you hand over all this documentation and that's it, right? Nope. There will be questions. Clarifications. Verifications. Your loan officer is trying to build a case that supports a decision to give you money; this requires a complete picture of you and your finances. If you missed a loan payment somewhere along the way, you'll be asked to explain and back it up in writing. If some bit of information is missing, you'll be asked to fill in that blank.

Be ready to explain anything that raises a lender's red flag, such as an unusually large collection of credit cards or bills, little or no credit history, having little or no down payment money, low credit scores, a combination of low base salary and high bills, or a reluctance to share information.

Thorough documentation gives a lender more evidence to support approving your application. Assuming the information is favorable, the more documentation you have, the better your chances for quick approval of your loan. Lots of favorable documentation means your application poses less risk for the lender. In return, the lender may reward you with, perhaps, a lower interest rate or other appealing terms.

What a Difference a Debt Makes

Debt (such as credit card and loan obligations) has a lot to do with how much lenders are willing to give you. A whole lot. Because while the lender is trying to decide how trustworthy you are, the company is also looking at how much more debt (in the form of your mortgage) you can take on given your current income.

Back in Chapter 4, I mentioned that for many loans, lenders typically assume that total monthly debt, including a new mortgage, should be no more than about 36% of monthly income. (For jumbo loans, loan officer Jean Keller says, it's about 42%.) For housing alone, the rule of thumb is about 28%. These numbers refer to the *Debt to Income Ratio*, or *DTI*.

The actual DTI your lender will apply to you may be higher or lower than the 36% and 28%, depending on the condition of your finances and credit. Whatever the number, the DTI your lender assigns to you is a finite box with sides that don't stretch. All your debts, including your house payment, will have to fit neatly into that box with room to breathe. The box can't be stuffed like a clown car with somebody's left leg sticking out the back window. So the more debt you have in credit cards, student loans, car loans and such, the less room you have for a mortgage payment. Here's an example from loan officer Kevin Mahoney:

Two buyers have \$5,000 monthly incomes. Based on that income, plus their other financial information, the lender decides that a 36% DTI is appropriate for both. They apply for the same type of mortgage with a 6% interest rate and a 5% down payment. Their applications are identical, with one exception: one buyer is carrying more debt than the other.

How will the difference in their debt burdens affect the loan amount each qualifies for?

	Buyer A	Buyer B
Monthly Income	\$5,000	\$5,000
36% Target DTI	\$1,800	\$1,800
Monthly Debt:		
Car	\$ 500	\$ 300
Loans	\$ 300	\$ 150
Credit Cards	\$ 200	\$ 90
Total	\$1,000	\$ 540
DTI so far	20%	11%

Buyer A has used up almost twice as much of the 36% DTI limit as Buyer B in loans and credit cards, leaving less room for a new mortgage. Using this information, the lender calculates monthly P+I for these potential buyers as follows:

	Buyer A	Buyer B
Monthly P+I	\$ 560	\$ 1,020
Tax, Insurance, Condo Fee	\$ 240	\$ 240
Other Debt (from above)	\$ 1,000	\$ 540
Total	\$ 1,800	\$ 1,800
DTI final	36%	36%
Maximum Loan Amount	\$93,400	\$170,000
5% Down Payment	\$ 4,915	\$ 8,950
Maximum Purchase Price	\$98,315	\$178,950

As you can see, because of the lower debt burden, Buyer B qualifies for a substantially higher loan amount than Buyer A and still has a DTI that doesn't exceed 36%. There will be a lot of factors determining your maximum loan amount, so even if you have the same income as the buyers in the example, your maximum won't necessarily look like theirs. But the point of these examples is that having a lot of debt can cost you the house you really want.

Keep in mind that your application isn't exactly final until you're ready to buy. So any debt you add between your initial application and settlement can be noted and included in the calculations of your loan amount. Additional debt added after you make an application for a loan amount may change the amount of cash your lender is willing to send your way.

But Wait, There's More!

Your lender has examined every last detail of your finances and has qualified you for a loan based on a DTI that suits you. All set, right? Hold up, not so fast. When the lender makes that calculation, what gets included in the debt category? Things like student loans, car loans, credit cards and such. What's missing? You still have to eat!

You have expenses that aren't a part of the debt calculation. Food and clothing. Childcare. Utilities, phone bills, toys for the kids, your annual vacation. Yes, some of these are wrapped up in your credit card bills, and lenders do look at your tax forms. But they don't include in their calculations every single thing you'll ever spend money on.

Before you take that $300,000 loan offered you, add your $50,000 down payment, and buy a $350,000 house, think about all those other expenses. How does your complete financial picture look? Can you take on a $300,000 loan and still stick to your financial goals? Still want to send the kids to summer camp? Still want to feed them when they return home? Include all those other expenses as you assess the monthly impact your new mortgage payment will have on you, your family, and your lifestyle. When it's time to buy your home, base your buying decision on a review of your whole picture, not just what you might qualify for. Remember, you have a choice. Just because you qualify for $300,000 doesn't mean you have to use it all. Use what works for you.

Now that you've figured out your finances, pre-qualified for a mortgage, and have a down payment sitting in your bank, it's time to spring into action. Time to find a house!

II

RELEASE THE HOUNDS!
THE HOUSE HUNT

When I started hunting for House #1, I made a mistake. I didn't give enough thought to what I wanted. I was looking for something not too far from work or shopping. Two bedrooms. Enough room for my stuff (not a lot to ask, given that I'd been living in an apartment). That about covered it. But when I started roaming around with a real estate agent, my criteria weren't very helpful. It wasn't that easy to pinpoint any one place as "mine."

Had I been more prepared, I could have told my real estate agent that I needed *these* features in my new home, but not *those*. Some of *that* would be nice, though I wouldn't fall into a deep depression if I didn't get it. With a longer list of "this" and "that," my agent would have had a better idea of what to show me. As it was, we saw so many two bedrooms near my job and shopping, I couldn't remember them all. The details of one house started blurring into the details of another because I hadn't worked out a way to sort through them all efficiently. I figured out what I wanted as I was looking.

When house hunting, a little preparation goes a long way. In my searches for Houses 2 through 5, I benefited from getting my thoughts in order before starting the search. As a result, I made much better use of my agents' expertise.

In this section, you'll learn to:
- Decide what kind of house and features you need and want
- Choose and work with the right real estate agent
- Organize your house hunting results
- Narrow your choices to find the right house for you!

7

THE WISH LIST

What kind of house do you need? What kind do you want? Hoping for a nice home without a huge yard to maintain? Maybe townhouse life is the thing for you. Have a spouse, five kids, three dogs, two cats, and a grand piano? A 1,000-square-foot condominium might not be in your future. Once you know your loan and down payment amounts, you'll know what kind of price range you can afford. Now it's time to match your price with housing choices that suit you.

Choosing the house that's right for you begins with listing the features you'd like it to have. Develop a Wish List that includes everything you hope to have and pinpoints things you want to avoid. To start, think once again about the role your house will play—long-term family home, investment to live in, and so forth. If you know you're going to sell in a few years, factor into your decisions things that will be appealing to other buyers when you resell the place.

Next, decide what features you will and will not consider. You'll find that some things are a definite for you ("We need at least four bedrooms."), and other things you'll remain undecided on until you see what's out there ("I'm thinking either a townhouse or a condo."). So let's get your list started.

Location, Location, Location, and Location, Too

Location is *that* important. A house on a quiet street with attractive neighboring houses and trees lining the back will likely have a higher price than the same house facing a busy street and a store with a steady stream of loud delivery trucks rattling around.

Location makes a big difference when it comes to the appeal and value of a house. The house itself might be perfect, but what if it's in an area that doesn't meet your needs? It's important to know what areas appeal to you. Would you prefer the city, suburbs, or country? How close do you want to be to work, schools, entertainment, shopping, and public transportation? If you have kids, are there places for them to play? What else is important to you?

A House by Any Other Name

Once you've chosen a location, the next step is the house itself. Where to begin? When you think about your family, your lifestyle, and your daily routine, what kind of house will fit the bill for you? The answer depends on how much ownership and responsibility you want to take on, how close you want to be to your neighbors, how much space you need. Here are the most common options:

Single Family Home. This is what we traditionally think of as a "house." It sits by itself on a piece of land, unattached to anyone else's house. Your neighbors are no closer than the edge of your property. You own the entire house and the land that comes with it. And you have sole responsibility for all maintenance, repairs, and emergencies.

Townhouse. This is a multi-level home attached to other townhouses on each side, forming a row. You share both side walls with your neighbors (unless you have an end unit, in which case you share only one wall). You own:

- everything inside
- the exterior of the non-shared walls
- the shared walls until you reach the *firewall*—the "core" of the shared wall, made of cinderblock or some other material—that helps prevent fire from spreading from one unit to another
- the roof
- usually a deck, patio, and/or small patches of land directly in front of and behind the unit

Everything else within the community is common area co-owned by you and the other owners. In addition to your own utilities, you pay a monthly fee to a homeowners' association for property maintenance and management of the common areas. There is also a set of policies that all owners and tenants must abide by, usually covering things that help promote safety and maintain the value of the properties in the community. There's no landlord, but you can contact the homeowners' association for help with issues related to the common areas and policies.

Condominium. This a single- or multi-level home attached to other units, either apartment or townhouse style. You own everything inside up to the interior walls. The rest of the building and the land are co-owned by you and the other owners, and the care of the buildings and grounds is governed by a community management organization. You pay a monthly fee to this organization for property maintenance and management.

Some utilities may be included in the fee, but you pay for the rest yourself. For example, a condominium community may include water in its fee, but owners must pay their own electricity and other utilities. As with a townhouse, there are policies that condominium owners and tenants must live by. While there's no landlord, the community management organization hires a property management company to take care of issues related to the common areas. Of these three types of houses, a condominium is closest to apartment life because of the more limited ownership.

A Plot of Land. If you're daring enough to start from scratch, somewhere in the world there is a special plot of land just waiting for you to build your dream house on it. You buy the land, hire the contractors, pay all the construction costs, and go for it.

Something Old, Something New, Something Cozy with a View

Here's another choice: Would you rather buy a house that's already owned and standing or go for new construction and be the original owner? Which is best depends on how much time and effort you're willing to invest and the extent of your imagination. Of my five houses, three were resales, two were new construction. They all had their moments.

Resale. This is a house someone else has owned. A known entity, you can see it, walk through it, see how much light streams through the windows, and touch it to see if anything falls apart. What you see—and what your home inspector finds—is what you get, including carpet, cabinetry or some other feature you might not have chosen if the decision had been left up to you. Sure, you might hate the wallpaper in the bathroom, but you won't be standing out in the cold, staring at a partially-built house wondering when it'll be done.

If you buy resale, in what shape are you willing to accept it? Do you want to be able to simply move your stuff in and go about your business (translation: save time and stress), or are you willing to work on repairs and improvement projects (translation: save money on the sale price)? "Work" can mean anything from removal of that hideous wallpaper, fresh paint, and a few minor repairs you or a handyman can handle, to major remodeling and construction. "Major" is always defined as expensive and time-consuming.

New Construction. Compared to a resale, new construction takes much more imagination. You stand in the middle of a dirt pile, look around, and say, "Yep. I can live here." In a *planned community*, where an entire neighborhood of houses is created, the builder is kind enough to provide model homes to show you finished samples in all their glory. Models are professionally decorated and loaded with plenty of extras to give you lots of interesting ideas. Just remember that when yours is done, you'll be staring at the plain white walls of a big, empty box.

But the fun part about new construction is you get to choose some or even most of your new house's features. Well, it's fun if you like this sort of thing. Do home improvement shows make your heart go pitter-patter? If so, you'll love this. But if you hate the idea of decision after decision about every last detail, think twice about new construction.

Musts, Wants, Nice-to-Haves, and Nevers

Time for the details—the features inside and outside of your future house. The trick here is to match

chartattack!

In **Chart E** in the Appendix, note your reasons for buying and which location and house types you'll consider. If resale is an option for you, also note what condition your new house should be in.

your lifestyle with the variety of home types in your target area. So organize your thoughts into the next part of your Wish List: Musts, Wants, Nice-to-Haves and Nevers.

- **Musts** are the things you cannot do without. ("Does it have enough bedrooms for everyone?")

- **Wants** are non-essential features you really want but can live without if you absolutely have to. ("We'd much rather have a two-car garage, but we can make do with a one-car.")

- **Nice-to-Haves** are extras you'll welcome if the house happens to have them. ("Hey, look. A fireplace in the family room. How nice.")

- **Nevers** are things you don't ever want to see in any home of yours. ("What's *that* doing here!? No. Just...no.")

So what are all those features out there? There are plenty, and you may be surprised at the variety you'll find as you hunt your way around town. Here's a sample platter:

- *Outside.* Exterior (siding, brick, stucco, wood), garage or carport, front and back yard, size and type of land, recreational facilities

- *Inside.* Number and sizes of bedrooms, number of full and half bathrooms, type of kitchen, other rooms, basement/ attic, appliances, décor, closet and storage space, fireplaces, unique features

One buyer's "Never" is another buyer's "Want." What's important to you? Chances are you'll modify your list a bit after you've seen a few places. Sometimes during the house hunt, you see a feature you hadn't thought of before. Or that

chartattack!

Use **Chart F** in the Appendix to mark your Musts, Wants, Nice-To-Haves, and Nevers. Add to, subtract from, or change the list to your heart's content.

fireplace idea just might grow on you, you know? Suddenly you have to have it! Add it to your list.

A Wish List Test Drive

Before you finalize your lists, it's a good idea to see if your wishes match your budget. For some ideas, take a look at *listings*—descriptions of houses available for sale—in free booklets, in newspapers, and on real estate websites featuring homes available across the country. Once you navigate your way to the cities you're interested in, the websites can be a particularly helpful way to get a good idea of what's available at what prices. Many of the websites include filters that allow you to limit your search to homes within your price range and with some of the features from your lists. You'll end up with a set of listings that most closely match your criteria.

Keep in mind, though, that because of the time lag between activity on a house and an update appearing in publications and on the websites, some of the houses you see may have already been sold. Also, not every available listing will be there. But you can still give your Wish List a good workout.

What do you think? Are you being realistic? Can you get what you want within your price limits? Maybe a certain combination of features just isn't available in your price range. Are you willing to let something go? Think it over. While you're at it, print or cut out any listings that look particularly interesting or at least are similar to what you want. You can use these later to help explain your needs to your real estate agent.

Price and the Real Estate Market

When you look at listings, the price you'll see is the *list price*— a starting price the seller is asking for the house, subject to nego-

What's Online?

The National Association of Realtors® owns a website containing a wide variety of listings:

- www.realtor.com

What's in Print?

Free booklets containing local listings can be found in supermarkets, train stations, and other public locations.

tiation. The condition of the real estate market has plenty to say about that price and how negotiations will go. If there are a lot of houses on the market but only a handful of buyers looking at them, it's a *buyer's market*. Buyers can be picky and more demanding, because there's not much competition to deal with. And sometimes they can get a house for less than the list price.

But if there are a lot of buyers and not enough houses to go around, it's a *seller's market*. Several buyers are more likely to compete for the same house, and sellers can expect a higher price and fewer demands from buyers. If you're in a seller's market, it's possible that you'll have to go above the list price to get the house. It can even happen in a buyer's market if the house is particularly popular among buyers. So if you're looking at houses with list prices at the very top of your price range, you've left yourself no room to negotiate a higher price. You might have to walk away. Be prepared.

When you know how much you can afford, and you have an idea of what you're looking for in your new house, you're ready to talk specifics with a real estate agent.

TEAM CAPTAIN:
THE REAL ESTATE AGENT

O f all the professionals you'll work with in the home buying process, the real estate agent is key. Good real estate agents do much more than take you around town and show you a bunch of houses. They work closely with you, sometimes for months, to help you find the right place at the right price. They become an invaluable source of information, advice, and market expertise.

Notice I said *good* real estate agents. It's worth being redundant here to remind you that, as with any profession, there's good and bad. The agent you choose will have an important impact on your buying experience. Remember, you're looking for the house you'll live in for the next several years, if not the rest of your life, so it's critical to choose your agent wisely.

First, give yourself time to make the right decision. You don't want a situation where you start working with one agent, see some houses, and discover things aren't working out. You don't have to stay with an agent if you're not satisfied with him or her. But if you choose a second agent after you've started working with the first, things will get complicated. If you decide you like a house you saw with the first agent, that first agent may have a legal right to the commission. Meanwhile, the second agent will be none too happy about that state of affairs. And, frankly, the first one won't be too happy either, after being replaced. Don't put yourself in that situation. Do some extra work up front to select an agent you feel comfortable with, and save yourself some agony.

Signs of a Good Agent

A good real estate agent knows how to turn your Wish List into the right house for you. She or he will:

- get to know you well enough to understand what you need and want in a house

- keep current on what houses are available and notify you when something new goes on the market

- find houses for you through his or her connections with other real estate agents

- once you find a house, explain the sales contract and how it works

- advise you on what should and should not be included in the sales contract

- answer your questions about the home buying process

- if you need it, help you find a mortgage lender, home inspector, or other professionals

- provide information about the locations you're considering

- advise you concerning issues you may face should you decide to resell the place in the future

- return your phone calls within a reasonable period of time

- help you keep your expectations realistic

A good real estate agent will *not*:

- be difficult to reach

- dismiss your concerns

- pressure you to buy his or her own listing

- disappear after the contract is signed and only reappear
  at settlement

- show you houses that don't match your most important criteria

- refuse to show you houses you're qualified to buy

Acronyms and Other Credentials

Real estate agents often hone their skills with additional courses
and training. Susan Corcoran, Associate Broker, explains some of
the credentials you may see next to a real estate agent's name:

- *GRI.* Graduate of Real Estate Institute

- *CRS.* Certified Residential Specialist (focuses on the
  residential market)

- *CBS.* Certified Buyer Specialist (focuses on representing
  buyers)

- *Broker or Associate Broker.* An agent with additional training
  in investment and law, so has the credentials to open up
  his or her own company

- *Realtor*. A member of the National Association of Realtors®
  who agrees to conduct business in accordance with the
  association's code of ethics

Some agents also have credentials that refer to their sales volume. The meaning of these numbers will vary depending on
where they are and what kind of houses they're working with. If
an agent has sold, say, $10 million worth of houses in a year, would
that mean more houses in a small rural area then it would in New

York City? A few big ticket houses or a lot of less expensive ones? So there's something to ask about.

Personality Matters

When choosing a mortgage lender, home inspector, or title company, personality is not the highest priority. But when it comes to choosing a real estate agent, personality really does make a difference. Because you will be joined at the hip for days or weeks during the house hunt, it sure helps if you like each other! But more importantly, personality matters because your real estate agent can best help you when he or she truly understands you and your particular situation very well.

When selecting a real estate agent, you need someone you can trust and work with comfortably. You need someone who will skillfully guide you through what, at times, will feel like a confusing maze. If you're buying for the first time, you especially need someone who's patient and willing to answer all those questions you will have. You need someone who is compatible. I like to approach the whole process in a systematic, strategic manner (You'd never know by reading this book, would you?), so the best agents for me work in the same manner. What's compatible for you?

I'm fortunate. Most of my agents were great to work and spend time with. I learned that one of my favorite agents absolutely adored grilled cheese and tomato sandwiches and another had a thing for the Beatles, especially George. The real key, though, wasn't their hobbies and preferences. It was that each agent listened well, took the time to learn about me and my life, and made things happen.

But I did meet a couple of real estate agents with whom I clashed. On one occasion, I stuck with the agent, not realizing that I really didn't need to. I eventually found what I needed, but it wasn't the most pleasant experience. Okay, it was miserable. I learned my lesson from that experience and conducted some interviews before jumping into later hunts. (Interviews are discussed below.)

Finding Candidates for the Job

There are thousands of real estate agents out there. How do you narrow down the possibilities? First, ask around. Ask your home-owning relatives, friends, and co-workers for recommendations. This may be all you need to do to find the perfect real estate agent. Perhaps one agent stands out from the crowd with the most glowing recommendation from someone you know and trust. If that's the case, great! You're in luck. But don't skip an interview to make sure that agent is right for you, too.

But it might take a little more work to find the ideal agent. You can contact area real estate companies and ask to speak to an agent. Be careful, though; this "cold call" approach may be too random to get you what you really need. So be specific. For example, can you work with a newer agent who may have more time to devote to you (which may be a trade off for lack of experience)? Do you prefer the top agent in the office? Maybe someone who specializes in your geographic area? Whatever your priorities, express them when asking for an agent.

Another approach is to look up area agencies online and zero in on the ones with plenty of experience and successes. Gail Belt, Realtor®, suggests contacting the local area Board of Realtors® to ask for a list of top agents, and going to open houses advertised in local newspapers to find agents who dominate in the areas you're interested in. She also suggests sticking with full-time professionals only and checking their websites to determine their level of experience and expertise.

Once you have a few names (and you really only need a few; don't go crazy and call the world), contact them and arrange a separate meeting with each one. There's no fee just for meeting with an agent. Fees come in later and are described in the next section.

The Interviews

When setting up your meetings, explain that you're talking to a few agents and will choose one after you've met with everyone. You want to be fair to the agents and let them know what's going on. If possible, these should be face-to-face meetings, not phone meetings; you need to assess compatibility, and that's harder to do over the phone.

Now for your interview. Plan about an hour for each. Agents typically have brief presentations to show you what they've accomplished for their clients and what they can do for you. They should ask you about your needs and wants: type of house, area you're interested in, price range. If you already have your Wish List, it'll be easy for you to summarize what you're looking for.

Ask questions that will give you enough information to choose the best agent out of the group. Here are a few to get you started. Some may be answered in the agent's presentation.

- *How long have you been in real estate?* Experience sure can help.

- *How long have you worked in this area?* You want someone who knows his or her way around the area and who can spot houses that may be right for you.

- *How many buyers have you worked with in my price range? What was the outcome?* Realtor® Gail Belt suggests asking this question to help you find someone who has successfully helped buyers like you.

- If this applies to you: *Have you worked with many first-time buyers?* First-time buyers need more information, explanations, guidance, and time to figure things out. Is the agent prepared for this?

- *What is your role in the home buying process?* The agent should be an advisor, spokesperson, and source of information for you through the house hunt, contract negotiations, home inspection, problem solving, and settlement.

- *What is my role in the process?* The agent should expect you to be clear about your needs, wants, concerns, and questions.

- *Do you have client references? May I contact them?* The best endorsement: a happy homeowner.

- *Do you charge a transaction or retainer fee?* Susan Corcoran, Associate Broker, suggests asking this question because some agencies charge these fees for their services, some of which must be paid up front (a retainer).

- *Can you provide an estimate of closing costs for my price range?* It'll be a ballpark figure, but it will help you prepare your finances.

After the last interview, take some time to compare your notes for each agent. Which one do you think best "gets" you and is most likely to be there from the time you agree to work together to the moment you get the keys to your house? Is this someone you can trust? Someone you can spend hours with riding around in a car, going from house to house, talking about what you like and don't like? Someone who can keep you calm without administering medication?

Once you've chosen a real estate agent, call the lucky winner and start making plans. And don't forget to call the others, thank them for their time, and explain that you've chosen to work with someone else.

By the way, if you're eligible for your employer's relocation benefits, you'll probably get a list of agents from the company participating in the relocation program. But what if you want to work with someone else? Check your relocation policy and talk to your relocation representative to find out what effect that will have on the benefits your receive from your employer.

You Have an Agent! Now What?

Once you've chosen your agent, it's time to get to work! First, your agent will give you a *buyer/broker agreement* or *buyer's agency agreement*—a form stating that the agent represents you, the buyer, and not the seller. It means the agent will be working with your best interests in mind. This is a contract, Associate Broker Susan Corcoran says, and it should include some kind of time limit and explain your rights to end the relationship if you're not satisfied. Here are a few other things to be aware of and watch for in a buyer/broker agreement or buyer's agency agreement:

Dual Agency. This happens when one agent represents both the buyer and the seller. In some states, it's also when one agency represents both parties (e.g., two agents within the same real estate company). In other states, that second situation may be called *designated agency*. If you run across this issue, ask yourself how well your interests can be represented if one agent is representing both you and the seller.

Fees. As I mentioned in the interview section, some agencies charge *transaction fees*, sometimes including a retainer you pay when you start working with the agent. These fees may be negotiable, Susan Corcoran says, so ask.

Commission. On the day you finally buy your house, your agent will earn a *commission*—a percentage of the price of the house. You won't write a check for this yourself; it'll be paid out of closing costs (covered in Chapter 13).

Again with the Wish List

At this point, your most important job will be to teach your agent about yourself. This should be easy, because you will have your Wish List and maybe a few sample listings to help you communicate some of your interests to him or her. Tell the agent as much as you can about your family, your lifestyle, your work, schools your children attend, and anything else you think is important. If you're on the fence about some features you'd like your new home to have ("We can't decide between two bedrooms or three."), say so. Your agent will plan to show you both options or help you rule one out.

With your Wish List and the other information you provide in your discussion, your agent can start finding the right listings for you to see. Get prepared to take the show on the road!

9

HOUSE HUNTING TRIPS: ARE WE THERE YET?

And now for the action/adventure part of our program—the house hunt. You're about to make a difficult decision. Way back in the first chapter, I called this a business transaction that will affect you financially for years. But it's also a practical and emotional decision. You will have to juggle three different concerns throughout the process:

Your financial needs. As discussed in earlier chapters, your choice must be compatible with your finances.

Your lifestyle. You've been dreaming of a garage with plenty of space for all your tools and projects. You travel a lot and don't want much to maintain. Your oldest son is now ready to have his own room. The kids have all moved out. Which house will support your kind of life? If you've worked hard on your Wish List, a good portion of your work is done. But once you start looking at houses, you can expect to review some of these criteria again as you see homes with attractive features you might not have considered before. Keeping yourself focused on your true needs will be a constant challenge.

Your emotions. You'd be surprised how the littlest things can stir your feelings as you look at potential houses. A cool gadget in the kitchen can grip your attention and have a bigger influence on your decision than you realize. Or a tree in the back yard gently swaying just so can pull you right back to your childhood home. With every house you see, you'll come away with an overall idea of how it makes you feel. And those feelings will have a powerful influence on the home you select.

So how do you keep all three decision beanbags in the air and end up in the right house? The best way to help yourself through this is to take your real estate agent interview process, your Wish List, and your analysis of your finances seriously. Get prepared.

Hunting Season

So how long will it take to find your new house, anyway? It depends on the real estate market, what's available within your price limit, any time constraints you have, and how picky you choose to be. Ask your agent about the inventory of houses in your price range and how long those listings are likely to stay on the market. In a seller's market, houses can get snatched up pretty fast, sometimes even on the day they're placed on the market. In a buyer's market, houses are more likely to stay on the market long enough for the "For Sale" sign to sway in the wind. If you're incredibly lucky, you'll find something on your first day out. But typically, it can take days or weeks. Sometimes longer. Yes I know, I know.

Listings

The hunt begins with a *listing*—a description of a house for sale. The *listing agent*—the real estate agent the seller hires to help sell the house—registers the property with the real estate industry's *Multiple Listing Service (MLS)* —a service that maintains information on houses for sale. The resulting description typically includes:

- A photograph of the house

- Price

- Address

- Owner name and contact information

- Listing agent's name, agency, and contact information

- Square footage

- Number of levels

- Age of the house

- Rooms and their approximate dimensions

- Townhouse or condominium community information and fees

- MLS identification number

- Annual property taxes

- Utilities

- Public school district

Listings also highlight features that *convey*—that are included in the sale—as well as appealing features ("Has new carpet and state-of-the-art appliances!") and special instructions ("Call first." or "Don't let the cat out!"). Your agent has access to these MLS records and will pull several that are potential matches for you.

Sometimes when you go to a house, you'll find that the selling agent has left a sales package consisting of not just the listing, but more detailed descriptions and pictures, community information, a list of improvements the sellers made, and maybe even a floor plan. By all means, take one before you leave. The more information, the better.

Your House Hunting Kit

You're going to be spending several hours traveling around in your agent's car, looking at house after house. Prepare yourself with a few things to make the day easier.

- *A clipboard and pen.* You'll need to keep your listings organized and make notes about each house you're seeing. If you don't, I promise you they'll all start to blur together in your mind by the end of the day.

- *Your Wish List.* Compare each house to your list.

- *A tape measure.* If you see a house you really like, will your furniture fit?

- *An area map.* Your agent may give you one, or you can bring your own. Use it to plot the location of each house. And if you reach the middle of the day and find that you're all turned around, use it to ask your agent where the heck you are!

Planning the House Hunting Day

You and your agent will agree on a day and time to start your hunt. A house hunting trip can take a full day, a half day, an evening after work, or whatever you and your agent arrange. It's not uncommon to spend a whole day looking at homes. In any case, make sure you're dressed for the weather and prepared for a lot of walking.

On hunt day, you'll meet at your home or hotel, or the agent's office, and review the listings for the houses he or she plans to show you. After answering your questions, the agent will call the sellers or listing agents to either ask to see the properties that day or leave a message stating that you'll be visiting. Then you're off!

First Impressions

On the way to each house, review its listing so you'll know what to expect. As you approach, take a look at the things you pass along the way. What do you see? Businesses? Parks? Neighborhoods? Do the surroundings appeal to you? Jot down any thoughts on the listing page.

When you arrive at the house, take a look around outside. Does the house look to be in good shape? Does it have the space you want? How do the neighbors' homes look? See anything you don't like? Make notes.

In most areas, there's a small lockbox, containing the house key, somewhere on or near the front door. For obvious security reasons, only real estate agents will have the codes to open it. You cannot enter a house without an agent. In case the seller happens to be home, the agent will knock or ring the doorbell first. If no one's there, the lockbox will serve its purpose. Associate Broker Susan Corcoran adds that in areas where lockboxes are not used, your agent will have to rely on the selling agent to let you both in.

Most of the time, sellers will not be home. If they are when the agent calls ahead of time, they'll probably leave before you arrive. Most selling agents recommend that sellers leave when potential buyers stop by. This gives you the comfort to talk to your agent without worrying about being overheard, and it keeps the seller from having to answer questions that the seller's agent should be answering.

Not all sellers take this advice, however. I've had a couple of instances where the seller insisted on following my agent and me around the house and pointing out all the wonderful features. I could barely hear myself think! It was annoying and just a little bit creepy. We didn't stay long. If this happens to you and it makes you uncomfortable, tell your agent. If the house interests you enough, you can always come back at another time when the seller's gone.

Picture This

As you move through the house, try to picture yourself, your family, your things living there. Can you imagine yourself relaxing in the family room? Will your kids have enough space to play? Will your stuff fit and look right in those rooms? Don't be afraid to open cabinet doors, peek inside the shower stall, stand inside the walk-in closet. After all, you might end up living there. Do your best to figure out what you'll be getting if you decide this is the house for you.

As you walk through the house, constantly share your thoughts with the agent—what you like, what you don't like, what concerns you, what you're not sure about, how the place compares to your Wish List. Be honest with your agent, and don't worry that something that's important to you seems trivial or silly. If you won't even consider a house unless it has separate sinks in the master bathroom, say so. If a balcony gives you traumatic flashbacks of having to portray Juliet in the eighth grade school play, say so. It's your life. Your money. Your home.

As you browse, let your agent point out things to consider and teach you about features that, in her or his experience, are desirable or could be problems. If you know you'll only be in the new house for a few years, discuss with your agent the things in and around the house that may affect your ability the resell the place. On the listing, note as much as you can so you'll remember what belonged to which house.

What's On TV?
There's a show on HGTV called *House Hunters*. You can watch real estate agents take buyers through the house hunting process. Note how the potential buyers comment on their likes and dislikes.

After you've seen enough, the agent will leave a business card, lock the door, and return the key to the lockbox. Then it's on to the next house.

Amateur Sleuth: Spotting Problems

If the sellers have done their job, the houses you're visiting should be neat, clean, and in good condition. The contents shouldn't distract your imagination. Unfortunately, this isn't always the case. In my hunting days, I've encountered hopelessly cluttered rooms, dirty bathrooms, wild paint colors or wallpaper, cracked walls, water-stained ceilings, unpleasant odors, and one horrifying spider web big enough to trap a cow and its first-born calf. You have to wonder about the decision to put a house in that condition on the market (and about the location of the entity that spun that web!).

These things, especially clutter, make it harder for you to see what the rooms really look like and whether they're right for your needs. And clutter may be hiding things that mean time and money for you after you move in. So you have a decision to make. You can try your best to overlook the mess and keep looking, or you can decide to cut your visit short and move on to other houses. It might be that the sellers' taste in décor doesn't match your own, or they're just plain messy. But some things you see during your house hunt can hint at potentially complicated, expensive problems.

Even if you're not a professional home inspector, there are some things that you can watch for. Lou Scerbo, home inspector, recommends keeping an eye out for the following red flags:

- large cracks in the walls

- water stains on the ceiling or walls

- dampness in the basement (you can sometimes see or smell it)

- drafty areas

- soggy spots on the lawn

- faucets producing water that's not clear or that has an odor

- cracks or burns on the kitchen counter (These are sometimes conveniently hidden by an innocent-looking cutting board. I've missed that one before.)

You won't always see everything; many a problem can be camouflaged by a fresh coat of paint. Just note what you do see; an inspector will be looking for more. Here's something to think over: If what you *can* see is in not-so-great shape, doesn't it make you wonder about the condition of the things you *can't* see? Not sure what to do? Ask your agent for his or her opinion. If you're still interested, a home inspection (covered in Chapter 11) will help you determine the extent of any problems.

One more thing to note is how long the house has been on the market compared to similar houses in the area. If others tend to sell within seven days but the one you're looking at has been listed for over a month, you have to wonder why. It could be due to a repair issue that's relatively easy to overcome or because of a major problem most buyers are trying to avoid. So inquire about how long the house has been on the market and add the answer to your decision making process.

Is New Construction on Your Wish List?

New construction takes a tremendous amount of time and patience. How are your nerves? With resales, you get what you get and you go from there. But with new construction, you have lots of choices, each an opportunity to make your house as "yours" as you can make it.

When I decided to buy my first new construction house, I didn't realize I'd be subjected to so many decisions and details. Remember those trips to the eye doctor where you try to read the letters against the wall while the doctor keeps changing the lenses? ("Do you prefer this, or this? All right. Which is better, this? Or this? Fine, fine. How 'bout this? Or…this?") Building a new home is like that. For me it was fun at first, but by the end I was sure that if they asked me to make one more decision, I would, without warning, spontaneously combust. So be prepared to spend your time mulling over many, many details.

Choosing a Builder. The builder you choose can mean the difference between a beautiful house completed on time without disturbing your peace of mind and a nightmare complete with delays, poor workmanship, and a strong desire for sedatives. Find out as much as you can about your potential builders: their reputation and credentials, what they've built in the area, any problems or lawsuits, the experience and reputation of the project supervisors. Your real estate agent can help you get the information you need. With the amount of money involved (*your* money!), I can't stress enough the need to do your homework here.

The Model. In planned communities, the builder usually gives you maybe three or four choices of floor plans that vary in square footage, features, and price. Because your potential house doesn't exist yet, the builder constructs samples—*models*—of each floor plan for you to browse. Most include a variety of extra features and professionally decorated rooms. You select the model that fits you best then choose a specific property.

Typically, planned communities are built in *phases*, where several units are built at the same time on a section of the property. If you're buying in an earlier phase, be sure to ask where the later phases will be built. What looks like a spectacular view today may be blocked tomorrow by the next set of homes going up.

Features. Without further adieu, I present...the fun part! Features! Which do you get to choose? If you're building a custom home, almost everything. In planned communities, the builder will give you several items from which to choose.

Now here's the catch. There's always a catch, isn't there? In a planned community, some of the things you can choose are ***standards***—things *included* in the base price of the house (such as a choice of flooring, cabinet finishes, and countertop surfaces)—while others are ***options***—upgraded or extra features that *add* to the price of the house (extra rooms higher quality fixtures, etc.).

While you're choosing, be careful. It's easy to get swept up in the joy of all the extras and gadgets and what not. If you don't keep your wits about you, this can easily turn into the Biggest! Shopping Spree! Ever! Choose too much, and suddenly you've "optioned" yourself out of your budget—and out of a potentially good house.

If you choose an option, make sure it's worth the extra money. After all, if you can't cover it in your down payment, it will add anywhere from a few hundred to several thousand dollars to your mortgage. Consider these questions:

- Does it have to be installed before the drywall goes up?
- Would it involve moving the walls around?
- How much effort would it take to do after you move in?
- Can you do without it?
- Is it likely to be significantly more valuable than the standard feature if you resell the house?

Talk it over with your agent. Whatever you choose, the base price plus the cost of options will have to fit within your price limit.

Whoops! Builders are human like the rest of us, so mistakes are always a possibility. With new construction, a feature can be forgotten or the wrong one included. A wall can even end up in the wrong place (all the more reason to choose the right builder!). When you buy new construction, you can't just sign the papers then disappear until the place is ready for you to move in.

Be prepared to make time to check on things periodically. Get to know the supervisor. If you call ahead, he or she can escort you safely around the construction site and show you what they've done so far. The earlier you find and report a problem, the better. During site visits for my new construction houses, I found that one crew had installed the wrong bathroom fixtures, and another was starting on a feature I hadn't ordered and didn't want. These were easy for them to correct at that point.

Pictures. Susan Corcoran, Associate Broker, suggests taking pictures throughout the construction process. This way you'll know where things are, such as wiring and plumbing, after the walls go up. If you have work done years later, you can show the contractor the pictures to help locate things.

It's also fun to see the progress. ("Ah, yes, I remember when it was but a mere foundation. Those were the days!") Building a house from scratch can be a long wait, and it helps to be able to remind yourself how much has already been done while you're waiting to move in.

Debriefing

During a break or at the end of your hunting day, go over your thoughts about the houses you've seen so far. If any house is a definite "no" for you, cross out the listing and set it aside. Make sure your agent knows why you've eliminated it and why the others are still in the running. This will help the agent narrow the search and plan the next trip.

Another thing you can do, Realtor® Gail Belt says, is go back on your own to the areas you looked at to try out the rush hour drive, see what's nearby, and take a quick look around the neighborhood. You cannot go inside the houses without your agent and an appointment, so please don't show up at someone's door and ask to see just one more thing. No need to unnerve the sellers. But you can check out the playground down the street, look for convenient commuting roads, and try to imagine the general area fitting your lifestyle.

Open Houses

Open houses can be a fun, easy way to see some houses and give your Wish List a spin. On a typical weekend afternoon, houses for sale are on display, ready and waiting for a stream of buyers to try them on for size. During an *open house*, the selling agent acts as host as buyers wander through the house at their leisure.

Open houses are advertised in newspapers, online, and with bold signs and balloons pointing the way on nearby streets. You can attend with or without your agent. The selling agent will ask you to sign in, at which time you can identify your agent. You and the other visitors can then roam around just as you would on any other house hunting day. Direct any questions to the selling agent, because the seller will be camping out at a friend's house or a local shopping mall until the wild party's over.

If you happen to fall in love with a place during an open house and your agent's not with you, contact her or him right away. Open houses can end with several contracts from eager buyers. But if you don't have your own agent, be careful. If the selling agent becomes your agent to help you buy this house, you will have a *dual agency* situation (covered in Chapter 8).

chartattack!

Use **Chart G** in the Appendix to list your favorite houses and compare them to your Wish List.

Narrow Your Choices

After each house hunting day, you will have your copies of the listings of the houses you've seen, along with your notes, to think over. Compare what you saw to your Wish List. When you and your agent feel like you've seen enough (or you've exhausted the supply of houses), it's time to narrow down your set of listings. Of all the houses you saw, which compare best to your list? Which ones appealed most to your instincts? Be careful here. Make sure your heart doesn't override your bank account!

And the Winner Is...

Discuss the best ones with your agent and arrange to go see each of them again. Chances are you'll see things you didn't notice before. If you get there at a different time of day, you'll see how the lighting changes, notice a change in the neighborhood's noise level, and maybe even meet a neighbor or two. By the way, this is a good time to whip out that tape measure and make sure your furniture will fit.

When you're done with these second (or third) visits, you'll hopefully have one house on your list that stands out from the rest, and one or two others that you're reasonably sure can also make you happy. Congratulations. It's time to put an offer on the table!

GOING ONCE, GOING TWICE, SOLD!
THE CONTRACT AND SETTLEMENT

You finally found the right house. It won't stretch your budget to the point of persistent pain. It has all of your Musts and most of your Wants. Now, how do you get your hands on it?

When I reached this phase with House #1, I remember being overwhelmed. There were negotiations and tons of paper flying around needing my signature or initials "here, here, right here, oh and don't forget here!" There were so many things to remember—do this, do that, don't go to sleep because there isn't time. Through the whole thing I wondered when, oh when, was that house finally going to be mine? This can be an incredibly stressful point in the buying process, especially if it's the first time you've dealt with it. But knowing what's coming is half the battle.

So how do you stalk and pounce on that house, sending other buyers in search of other prey? For this process, in the place of retractable claws we have contracts (which, when you're done, won't have a retractable clause!). If you and the seller can work things out, the house is one giant step closer to being yours, and you can start preparing for your friendly takeover.

In this section, you'll learn to:
- Work your way through the contract and negotiations
- Prepare for settlement
- Get through the settlement
- Get settled into your new house!

10

PUT IT IN WRITING:
THE SALES CONTRACT

Your quest for that house you have your eye on will depend on the success of your *sales contract*—the document that spells out the conditions under which you will buy the house. You will get the process rolling by making an initial offer, and unless the seller accepts your first offer as is, the contract will become a work in progress. Then in a tennis match of offers and counter-offers, you should eventually (hopefully!) reach a mutually beneficial agreement.

Anatomy of a Contract

The contract form may vary a bit from region to region, but it is likely to include certain standard elements. It identifies the buyer, seller, real estate agencies, and the address and legal description of the property. It lists the features of the house and indicates whether they're included in the sale. These are things such as major appliances, window treatments, and security systems. There's also a section about the utilities as well as the condition of the equipment and systems in the house.

A large portion of the contract addresses the buyer's ability to pay for the house: price offered, proposed down payment, amount to be financed, and mortgage details. The rest of the contract covers the seller's and buyer's requirements, contingencies, responsibilities and other legal matters. Finally, the contract lists a proposed settlement date—the date you'll actually buy the house—and a date by which the seller must respond to the offer. Always ask about anything you don't understand. Each of these elements is discussed in more detail below.

New Construction Contracts. If you choose new construction, it's important to know that builders have their own contracts. Chances are you'll be able to negotiate very little here, if anything; you may have to accept the contract as is. All the more reason to choose a reputable builder. Realtor® Gail Belt stresses the importance of reviewing the contract carefully with your agent and attorney (if you use one) before you sign it.

Even if you can't change the document, you must understand what you're signing. Ask for clarification if there's anything you don't understand. If you feel you can't live with something in the contract, Gail Belt says, "it is worth at least asking the builder's agent to attach an amendment. If this doesn't work, your only options may narrow to either letting the house go or proceeding with your eyes open and a hopeful heart. Although most builder contracts are very one sided, most buyers who buy from reputable builders do end up with a positive experience."

Is There a Lawyer in the House?

Your real estate agent will advise you throughout the process of making an offer and submitting a contract. As the contract is a legal document, you can also choose to have an attorney review the details, recommend changes, and help you understand what you're signing. Using an attorney is common in some areas, infrequent in others. If you decide to use an attorney, ask for recommendations from your agent or other people you trust. Be sure to ask for someone who specializes in real estate.

The Price is Right...

The most important piece of the contract, and your first decision, is the price you're offering. Should you offer the list price, something less, or something more? If less or more, by how much? The answer depends on several factors.

Your Limits. You already know how much you have available for a down payment. You know how much your mortgage lender is willing to lend you. And you've already decided how much of that mortgage amount you can fit into your budget. So there's your maximum. Anything less is all the better.

The Market. As a starting point, your agent will show you the list prices and actual selling prices for similar houses recently sold in the area. How different are those prices? In a buyer's market, you'll have more of an opportunity to negotiate in your favor. If there's little or no pressure from other buyers, you might be able to get the house for less than the list price. However, if it's a seller's market and you're competing with others, you may end up making an offer above the list price.

The Competition. Is there another buyer with an eye on the same house? Several buyers? If so, you may have to outbid the others if you want that house. Again, remember your limits. If the bidding gets too high for your wallet, be prepared to walk away. This is a tough one. What if you've developed an emotional attachment to the place? You have to decide at what point it's no longer worth it to you.

If you're in a market where the winning offers are likely to go above the list price, consider limiting your hunt to houses with list prices somewhat below your limit. This will give you room to negotiate higher, if needed.

...But Can You Pay It?

In the appropriate section of the contract, your agent will write in your offered price then summarize your ability to pay that price: your down payment and mortgage.

Pre-Approval. Now it's time to go back to your loan officer and get a *pre-approval letter*—a letter stating that you qualify for the amount needed to buy the house. The letter can be written in one of two ways—it can disclose the full amount for which you've been approved, or it can simply state that you're approved for your offered price. If you actually qualify for more than what's needed to buy the house, which number should your letter use?

There are two ways to look at this. A letter that includes the full amount you qualify for can imply financial strength. A letter that includes only the amount needed for the house doesn't let the seller know how much more you can potentially spend. Either option can be helpful in negotiations. The best one for you will depend on your situation, so discuss it with your loan officer and agent.

Deposit (Earnest Money). At the time you make your offer, you'll need to include a *deposit*, or *earnest money*—an amount of money (typically between 1% and 3% of the sale price, Associate Broker Susan Corcoran says) that essentially shows that you're serious about buying the house. You write a check for this amount, payable to your agent's company. This amount will be held in an *escrow account*—an account that's usually non interest-bearing— and at settlement will apply toward your down payment and closing costs.

Wait! Before you write that check, ask your agent whether the money is refundable should the deal fall through. That's a lot of money to lose if it turns out you have to go find another house.

Featured Features

This section is similar to the features section in the listing. Your agent will mark the things that convey according to that listing. The difference here is that it's possible to also include things that exist in the house but that weren't originally included in the listing. This is your way of asking the seller to consider including them.

If you've fallen in love with the window treatments, for example, but you notice they don't convey, you can note in the contract that you'd like them included. Then you hope they survive negotiations.

If This, Then That: Contingencies

Contracts often include *contingencies*—conditions that must be met before you'll agree to buy the house. These will vary by region, but here are a few common contingencies:

Home Inspection. Most buyers ask for this. You'll want to know if there are any hidden problems in the house, and if there are, you'll probably want at least some of them fixed (covered in Chapter 11).

Sale of Your Current House. If you're relying on the sale of your current house to pay for the new one, your lender will require the sale as a condition of your new mortgage. But in some areas this contingency can make it extremely difficult to negotiate your contract. If it's an issue, one option to consider is to sell or at least have a contract on your current house before you make an offer on a new one, Associate Broker Susan Corcoran says. Talk this one over with your agent and loan officer to decide what will work for you.

Tests and Other Inspections. Your agent will know if any other test or inspections are required for your area and type of house. These may include such things as tests for radon or lead-based paint, and inspections of wells and septic systems. Requirements for these tests are included in the contract as needed. Your contingency may be that the house has to pass these tests or inspections.

Condominium or Townhouse Documents. Houses in communities with homeowners' associations have documents governing the property (budgets, rules, etc.). You'll get a chance to review these documents before you make an offer on a home in the community. The contingency here is that you can agree to abide by the rules. If you decide that you can't live with the rules, you can cancel the contract.

Other Changes to the Contract. Sometimes a buyer is advised to eliminate some other lines or a paragraph in the contract (thus, making it more buyer friendly). If you choose or are advised to change the contract in this way, be aware that this can make the seller very uncomfortable. You may have to decide whether the issue is worth complicating the negotiations.

Bargain Hunting: Negotiations

Once you and your agent have structured your initial offer to your liking, your agent will fill in the contract, attach copies of your pre-approval letter and deposit check, and deliver the package to the seller's agent. Then things get suspenseful. Will the seller love the offer? Hate it? Laugh at the absurdity of it all? Stay tuned! Generally, the seller will have a few days to mull over your offer and respond—either accept the contract as is or make a counter-offer.

That response will depend on any other contracts coming the seller's way, how much they sense you want that house, personality, and whether it's a buyer's or seller's market. If it's a buyer's market, you're in a much better position to make requests, and you might be able to get most of what you want. In fact, the seller might opt to add things such as features that weren't originally included or payment for new carpet to replace one in bad shape.

But if it's a seller's market, the seller might sit back and take more of an "as is" approach. If other buyers are right behind you, ready to snatch that house out of your clutches, you might not be in a position to ask for much, if anything. If the seller refuses to negotiate at all, you're faced with either accepting the house, problems and all, or resuming your hunt. Work with your agent to figure out what's best for you.

Chances are your negotiations will involve several rounds of back-and-forth. You won't be dealing directly with the seller; you'll both be working through your agents. It's like the telephone game:

- Your initial offer says you want the contract to include items A, B, C, and D.

- Your agent sends your offer to the seller's agent, who sends it to the seller.

- The seller decides to accept items A and B, but won't touch item C or item D.

- Word of the seller's decision travels from the seller to the seller's agent to your agent to you.

- You think it over and tell your agent to tell the seller's agent to tell the seller that you insist on C but will give up D.

- The seller accepts, tells the seller's agent, who tells your agent, who tells you.

The scenario above is just an example of the fun. No two negotiations are the same. You or the seller can dig in your heels and refuse to listen to anything remotely resembling a suggestion, or you can be civil and try to work something out. At some merciful point, you'll reach an agreement of some kind—to arrange your purchase or to walk away from each other forever. Assuming that your final agreement isn't to walk away, the agreed-upon items are added to or deleted from the contract. You and the seller both initial the contract. Then you go somewhere and relax, because your head hurts and you've earned a break.

But don't go far. There's more to do!

11

A "DOCTOR" IN THE HOUSE:
THE HOME INSPECTION

The home inspection, a contingency in many contracts, is a house's version of a complete physical exam. It's a detailed check of the structure and features of a house to determine their safety and working conditions. It's your opportunity to put aside your excitement about the home you might soon own and get a reality check before you put your money on the table. You'll find out what's working in your potential house and what's not, what's easy to fix and what could be a deal breaker.

Inspections are fascinating to watch. Each of my inspectors attacked those houses with enough gadgets and scrutiny to make a crime scene investigator weep with jealousy. They dragged themselves into crawl spaces, hoisted themselves into stifling attic spaces, measured this, prodded that. And they found things I never would have known to look for.

Lou Scerbo, home inspector, says that buyers typically see a house with two sets of eyes. Before they buy, they tend to see what they want to see. But after they buy, they're more likely to see what they really got. I know how easy it is to get so caught up in the excitement of a new house that you overlook even the visible ugly blemishes. Not to mention the hidden ones. That's where a home inspector comes in.

Finding a Home Inspector

Because this is simply yet another round of our favorite game, "How to Find a Professional," I'll keep this one short. You can find a good inspector by asking homeowner relatives, friends, or coworkers (the "happy customer" approach). Your real estate agent will know several. As always, some are better than others, so remember to ask questions of the person making the recommendation.

Once you have a name or two, you can call them and conduct a brief interview, if you'd like. Then before the inspection, find out what the fee will be for the house you're buying (your real estate agent will know what is customary). You'll usually need to pay that amount on the day of the inspection.

A Day in the Life of an Inspection

Once you've chosen an inspector, you will work with your real estate agent, the inspector, and the seller's agent to schedule a time for the inspection. The seller will usually arrange to be out of the house. Depending on the size and condition of the house, the inspector will need anywhere from one to six hours. And so will you, because you get to follow along and watch!

At the time of the inspection, you will meet your real estate agent and the inspector at the house. The agent will either stay just long enough to unlock the house and get things started or stay for the whole thing. If for some reason you can't be there, the agent will usually fill in for you. It helps if you

chartattack!

On **Chart C** in the Appendix, add the inspector's fee.

can be there, though, so you can learn about the workings of your potential new house.

What Gets Inspected. Your inspector will have a long list of things to scrutinize. One thing you'll hear about is *settling*—houses shift over time as a result of moisture, temperature, and other natural factors. You'll see the effects of settling in every house, from new construction to the oldest houses. But there's so much more to look for. Here's a sample inspection list from home inspector Lou Scerbo:

Inspecting...	Looking for...
Walls and ceilings	Cracks, water damage
Windows	Cracks, proper opening and closing, locks, sticking
Doors	Sticking, settling
Closets	Settling
Insulation	Adequate coverage
Ventilation	Proper regulation of heating and cooling, condition of roof, comfort
Electrical service	Switch box and all switches and outlets in proper working order, compliance with applicable regulations
Heating and air conditioning, water heater	Proper and safe working order, air flowing unobstructed to all vents, age of systems
Plumbing	Main water source and all faucets work properly, leaks, condition of pipes
Major appliances (that will stay with the house)	Proper and safe working order, age

Inspecting...	Looking for...
Exterior drainage	Condition, obstructions, water directed away from house
Exterior finishes	Damage, cracks
Roof	Leaks, age, condition

You, the Observer

As the inspector moves through the house, you can follow along and watch. He or she will occasionally stop and point something out to you—usually a problem or something that's in particularly good shape. You might also get a quick how-to about care and maintenance of a particular item. I was shocked at a serious problem one inspector showed me. It seems the wall oven had never been bolted to the cabinet it sat in. With one finger, he was able to tip the oven half way out of the wall. Imagine discovering that when removing a dish from a 400-degree oven!

Your inspector will run the washer and dishwasher, give the dryer a spin, fill the tub and watch it drain, open and close the automatic garage door, test the sump pump, turn on the heat or air conditioning (depending on the weather), and generally climb all over the place. Follow where you can, but no one will expect you to scramble on up to the roof or shimmy into the crawl space. The inspector can take care of those without you just fine.

When the inspection is over, your inspector will give you a quick summary of findings and answer your questions. Then your real estate agent will lock the house, and the sellers can get their worked-over house back.

What's Not Inspected

There are a few things the inspector cannot cover. Generally these are things that can't be seen: anything behind the walls, or an attic or crawl space with no means of access, Lou Scerbo says. If the roof is beyond a certain height (for example, not accessible with a 13-foot ladder), the inspector might get out a pair of binoculars and examine the roof from the ground. If the heating and air conditioning are separate systems, it's difficult to inspect each in the off-season. Air conditioning units, for example, may be damaged if turned on when it's less than about 60 degrees or so outside. Your inspector will let you know if there's anything that can't be included.

There's one exception to the behind-the-walls limitation. If you've opted for new construction, you can get a pre-drywall inspection while the house is under construction. In this case, the inspector can examine electrical wiring, plumbing and anything else normally hidden behind the walls.

What's On TV?
If you want to get a glimpse of what a home inspector does, tune in to *House Detective* on HGTV.

What's Online?
The American Society of Home Inspectors (ASHI) has inspection information online:
- www.ashi.org.

Diagnosis: The Inspection Report

A short time after the inspection, your inspector will send your real estate agent a written report summarizing his or her findings. Some inspectors travel with computers and printers, so you might even get your report on the spot. The home inspector's report will include comments on the condition of each system checked and a description of anything that is malfunctioning, missing, not meeting regulations, or otherwise in need of attention. When you get your copy, read it over very carefully. Has your dream house turned into a nightmare? Or is it still a sweet dream?

A Note About New Construction

If you're buying new construction, don't assume an inspection isn't necessary. After all, there are a lot of details and people involved in building one house. There are plenty of opportunities for things to break, be overlooked, and need adjustment. One of my new construction houses had a dysfunctional doorbell, a missing attic fan, and a scratched countertop that had to be remedied. Consider an inspection here just as you would for a resale house. In fact, you have a unique opportunity also to have a pre-drywall inspection done during a new construction.

With new construction, builders often offer a *warranty*. This means that after you buy, the builder will be responsible for certain repairs during that warranty period. At specified intervals, you'll have a chance to meet with the builder, create a list of things that need fixing (sometimes called a *punch list*), and get them done. And if you're willing to spend the money, you can have an inspector come back before your warranty meeting to see if anything else should be added to your punch list. You don't have to do this, but it might be helpful. My inspector found a few things I never would have seen myself.

What About Your Contract?

If you have a home inspection included as a contingency in your contract, this is the time to walk away from the purchase if the report shows that things are in such bad shape that you no longer want the house. But if the inspection results are acceptable to you and you're still in the game, you have some choices to make. You can request that the seller fix some or all of the problems identified in the report (the seller pays for it), or you can accept the problems as is and plan to take care of them yourself (you pay for it). The seller, in turn, can agree to your request, amend it, or refuse the whole thing.

How do you decide what to do? It's all about negotiation. If you choose to ask the seller to make repairs, the completion of these repairs will become part of your contract—you agree to buy the house if the seller agrees to those requests. How much you ask the seller to do depends on two things: the nature of the problems and the amount of leverage you have as a buyer. If a problem is simply cosmetic and/or relatively easy and inexpensive to fix, you might consider letting it go if the seller won't budge. Problems involving safety, structure, expense, or a high potential for significant damage need more careful consideration. You may have to wage a battle between your emotional attachment to the house and your sense of financial responsibility. Work it through with your agent.

Once you and the seller have agreed on what will be included in the contract, the seller will get those items repaired and give proof that those repairs have indeed been made (receipts, for example). Then you'll both move on to the next phase.

To Waive or Not to Waive

Sometimes buyers drop the inspection contingency when competition for that dream house is stiff and they want the house badly enough to take the risk. If you're considering buying a house without having a home inspection, think hard about the pros and cons of this decision. There are many problems that can go unnoticed by untrained eyes. Some of those problems can make the house not as "worth it" as you might have thought.

If you've ever seen the movie *Poltergeist*, you know things can go very, very wrong in a perfectly normal-looking house. Everything looks good on the surface, but somewhere there's a problem, sitting all smug and menacing and invisible, just waiting for the worst possible moment to make a general mess of things.

Your "poltergeist" might be a major plumbing problem (which can flood the house), termite damage (which can weaken the structure), a faulty heating system (which can start a fire, spew carbon monoxide, or just not heat the house), a leaking roof (which can lead to water damage), an unsafe appliance (which can cause fire or injury), or any number of other things. Will that house still be as appealing if you discover it'll cost thousands to fix things? Without the inspection, you won't know.

If you choose to waive the inspection contingency in your contract, another option is to still get an inspection for your own information. Even if you agree to accept the house "as is," at least you'll know if you're inheriting any problems. And even without a home inspection contingency in the contract, home inspector Lou Scerbo says, a standard contract will still have a clause stating that electrical, plumbing, and mechanics must be in good working order. But understand that this clause is still not the same as a thorough home inspection. Talk it over with your agent.

12

A PRE-SETTLEMENT TO-DO LIST

When you and the seller have agreed on the terms for purchase and signed a final contract, the keys will be all but in your hands. Barring any unforeseen disasters, you will know where you're going to live, how much it will cost, and when it will be yours. So you can just sit back, relax, and wait, right? Well, not quite. Even with the hard parts pretty much done, you still will have a few things to do before settlement day.

The Care and Feeding of a Loan

It'll be important at this point to keep in touch with your loan officer to make sure arrangements are underway for your money to be available on settlement day. If you haven't already done so by this time, talk to him or her about locking in your interest rate (covered in Chapter 5). Don't forget that until the house keys are in your hands, your lender will be watching your spending. You might want to think twice about buying that new car you've been stalking.

Good Faith Estimate

Not long before your settlement day, your loan officer will give you an estimate of how much money to bring to settlement for your down payment and closing costs. This is called a *good faith estimate*. Don't expect it to be exact; you'll get that from your title company when you get closer to the big day. But the estimate will help you plan.

Is There a Lawyer in the House (Part II)?

If you used an attorney for your contract, he or she can help you through settlement, too. Attorney Emory Hackman points out that an independent attorney represents only you (not the real estate agency or title company, for example) and will help you wade through all the forms and manage any problems that may pop up. Plan to keep him or her updated with all documents for review. Is there anything you don't understand? Ask questions.

Power of Attorney

If for some reason you cannot attend your settlement (this sometimes happens with corporate relocations, for example), you'll need to arrange for someone to make decisions and sign forms on your behalf. This can be your attorney, your real estate agent, or someone else you trust. You'll need to plan this well ahead of your settlement date so the necessary forms can be signed and the designated person can arrange to be present. The process for a closing through power of attorney varies from place to place, so ask your agent, attorney, or title company for help on how to proceed.

You also will need to notify your loan officer if someone else will be signing for you, Associate Broker Susan Corcoran says, because the lender may require that certain forms be signed by you and only you. You'll need to get those ahead of time, sign them, and return them before your settlement date.

Utilizing Utilities

That wonderful new house will need lights and hot water. And a phone line or two. And some way to use the stove. So jump on the phone and call the local utility service providers. Give them your new address and settlement date, and arrange for service to be put in your name as of that date. If you're not familiar with the providers in your new area, your agent will have the information you need. And don't forget to report your upcoming address change to the post office so that you can get your mail forwarded to the new house.

Who's Moving Whom?

Unless you've been living in a dormitory or maybe a small tent, you'll need some extra hands to get all your stuff into your new humble abode. If you have the time, energy, and patience for the do-it-yourself route, all you need to worry about is maybe renting a truck and getting everyone in one place on the right day. My cousin once moved all the way across country in a rented van, with a five-year-old, a cat, and two fish for company. Brave.

If, however, you're going to use a moving service, give yourself time to plan. Be careful with your choice. Reputable companies will take good care of you, but there are others who will gladly take your money and literally run. With your stuff. So (here we go again!), when you choose a moving company, base your selection either on the "happy customer" recommendations from friends and relatives, or ask your agent to recommend a company or two you can contact.

The moving company will have a representative talk with you. Discuss the things you'll need to move. Talk about your destination and your new house, such as the number of rooms and any staircases the movers will have to use. The representative will give you an estimate based on several factors, including:

- The distance of the move
- The amount of stuff you have
- Whether you want them to pack and/or unpack for you
- Whether you need to have your things temporarily stored between moving out of the old place and into the new

There also may be extra charges to move exceptionally heavy, bulky, or valuable items. Some things they may not move at all, such as plants, animals, household cleaners and hazardous materials that can cause spectacular damage in a very hot or very cold moving van. You may want to look into separate services for items that need special handling, such as pianos. And if you have pets, please, please, *please* get some advice on how to give them a trauma-free move.

Be sure to ask your mover about insurance. While in the hands of the movers, will your possessions be covered for loss or damage? If so, will they cover items you've packed yourself, or only those packed by employees of the company? If anything is damaged, destroyed, or lost in the move, what's the process for getting the item repaired or replaced? When you get the contract, read it over carefully and ask questions or seek advice before signing if there's anything you don't understand.

I've had an interesting mix of experiences with several movers. I've had furniture scratched and broken, a white sofa and chair that had been carefully wrapped in plastic and stored for months delivered in perfect shape, a missing ladder, quick and efficient packing and unpacking, a wet box of books (Books, of all things! Books!), and professional follow up to resolve problems. Get the best mover you can find and afford. It's worth it for the condition of your possessions and for the hassles you can avoid. Moving is stressful enough. Give yourself a better chance for some peace of mind.

chartattack!

On **Chart C** in the Appendix enter your estimated moving costs.

Title Company and Insurance

If you have a mortgage, insurance is required for your new house. Chapter 14 covers the details of the types of insurances you may need and how to get them. And in the final stretch of the purchase of your house, you'll work with a title company. The next chapter describes what this company does.

:13.

PROPER PROPERTY PROCUREMENT: THE TITLE COMPANY

The *title company*, also referred to as a *settlement company*, has the task of bringing your purchase to the finish line. Lilian Rodriguez, title agent and attorney, says the title company's primary roles are to verify the seller's rights to sell the property and to ensure that ownership is legally transferred to you. The title company's role begins after you have a signed contract and ends shortly after settlement.

Choosing Your Title Company

Ah. So we're back in familiar territory, yes? When looking for a title company, there's the tried and true "happy customer" (ask your friends and relatives) method, and you can ask your agent for recommendations. You may be offered a preferred title company and perhaps even some kind of incentive to use that company over others. You may want to accept that offer, but be aware that you don't have to. In fact, while a builder or agent can certainly recommend a specific title company, they cannot *require* you to use it. It's your right to choose the best title company for your transaction.

A Letter to You

About a week before settlement, your title company will mail you a letter outlining the upcoming settlement process and letting you know what you need to do to prepare. The letter usually covers things such as:

- *Photo identification.* You'll need this on the day of settlement.

- *Funds.* Be prepared to bring to settlement your down payment and closing costs as spelled out in the letter.

- *Mortgage and insurance.* The title company will need the contact information for your lender and homeowner's insurance company, plus proof that you've arranged for your new home to be covered by insurance.

- *Utilities.* The title company will remind you to arrange for these services to be put in your name.

- *Legal services.* If you have an attorney, put him or her in touch with the title company. If you don't have one, the title company will use its own attorney to prepare legal documents associated with the purchase of your house.

- *Power of attorney.* If you can't be present at the settlement, you'll need to give someone the right to sign legal documents on your behalf (covered in Chapter 12).

- *Title company's fee.* This amount will be included in your closing costs.

Titles vs. Deeds

Titles and deeds both refer to the same thing—ownership of the property you're purchasing. Having the *title* means you have the ownership rights to the property, while a *deed* is the physical, legal document that shows you have that right, title agent and attorney Lilian Rodriguez says. It officially transfers ownership from the seller to you. The title company's tasks before settlement are aimed at preparing the way for a problem-free transfer of that title to you.

The Title Search

Well before the settlement date, your agent will send to the title company a copy of the contract, or your lender will send a *title request*. These documents trigger a *title search*—research on the property's history of ownership. Through court documents, the title company will verify that the seller has the right to sell the property and that there aren't any other forgotten owners from way back when that might pop out of the woodwork and claim a legal right to your property.

Title searches aren't limited to older homes that have had decades to collect a string of owners. New houses are built on land that was in someone else's possession at some point. It's not unusual, for example, for an entire neighborhood to be built on what was once farmland. What if that farmer's great grandchildren were under the impression that they somehow inherited the land? You never know, and that's exactly the kind of information a title search is intended to uncover.

Lien. The title search might show that the seller has neglected to pay creditors, such as contractors or a homeowner's association. In this case, there may be a *lien* on the property—which means the outstanding debt is attached to the property. Until that debt is settled, the house can't be sold, and you will end up with a delay. But that's better than ending up with someone else's debt, right?

Easement. The search will also reveal any *easements*—rights someone else has to access some part of the property. You'll often find easements granted to utility companies, for example, whose pipes or power lines run through the property.

Closing Costs

Closing costs are a laundry list of fees associated with buying your house and processing all the paperwork. In preparation for your settlement, the title company gathers information from your mortgage lender, insurance company, and others involved in the transaction to calculate your closing costs. The result is a seemingly endless stream of fees associated with making the house yours. The exact items included will depend on your circumstances, but expect to see things such as:

- *Lender fees.* This covers your points, processing fees, and advanced payments for some portion of mortgage interest and insurance premiums.

- *Taxes.* Any taxes your lender requires you to pay in advance (e.g., a specified number of months' worth) may be due at closing. You'll reimburse the seller for taxes they already paid that cover the settlement date and beyond.

- *Homeowners' association dues and transfer fee.* Again, you'll reimburse the seller for fees already paid that cover the settlement date and beyond. There may also be a fee to transfer association membership to you.

- *Title company fees.* You'll pay the title company for the title search and processing, title insurance preparation, and other administrative fees.

- *Government recording fees.* You pay these fees to officially list you as the new owner of the property in state and local records.

- *Attorney's fees.*

- *Any additional fees that apply to you.*

The seller will pay their own smaller set of fees and the real estate agents' commissions.

What's That Number?

About that money you have to bring to settlement...where does that figure come from?

| The money you owe | − | The money already paid | = | The money you bring to settlement |

Money You Owe. This is your contract sale price plus the laundry list of closing costs outlined above.

Money Already Paid. This is money that will be in an escrow account on settlement day, including:

- *Your mortgage.* The title company will arrange with your lender for your loan to be available on the settlement date.

- *Your deposit (earnest money).* You paid this when you signed your contract.

- *Any other loans, credits from the seller, or other funds.*

Money You Bring to Settlement. You'll need your down payment plus enough money to cover the rest of what you owe.

The Big Check

The day before I bought House #1, I got a huge check from my bank to cover my down payment and closing costs. Unused to having that much of my own money in my wallet, I wandered around paranoid for the rest of the day. I can't tell you how many "what-ifs" ran through my head. Was I glad when settlement rolled around and I could finally hand that thing over and watch it buy me the key to my—*my*—very own house? You bet!

Make sure your "big check" is sitting in your bank account, resting up for the big day. When you're ready to put it to work, be sure to give yourself plenty of time to get the check processed.

Title companies usually ask that you bring a cashier's check or money order; don't assume they'll take a personal check. You may be asked to include a little more in your check to cover any last minute fees or adjustments that may come up, and you will get back any excess after settlement.

You probably won't need to be surrounded by armed guards in cool sunglasses while action-adventure theme music propels you to safety, but when you get it in your hands, *guard that check!* Sorry. Paranoia flashbacks.

:14:

INSURED AND ASSURED

T here are two types of insurance you'll need to deal with before
you complete your purchase: homeowner's insurance and title
insurance. A third insurance, private mortgage insurance (PMI),
will already be arranged by your lender if you have less than a 20%
down payment (covered in Chapter 5).

Homeowner's Insurance

If you have a mortgage, you're required to have homeowner's
insurance (the second "I" in PITI). Once you have a contract, a
mortgage letter, and a settlement date, call your insurance company
and plan coverage for your new house. If you're not sure what
insurance company to choose—say it with me—ask around (the
"happy customer" approach), ask your real estate agent to recommend one, or try the company that insures your car or the contents
of your apartment. In any case, look for an insurance agent who
will take the time to explain your policy and answer your questions
about what's covered and what's not.

If you've been renting until now, get to know the many differ-
ences between renter's insurance and homeowner's insurance.

Jonna Wooten, insurance agent, explains that renter's insurance covers the replacement value of your personal possessions, such as clothing, furniture, and dishes, up to the policy limit. The building you live in is the responsibility of the people who own it. But when you buy, your responsibility includes the part of the property you own. For single family houses, that's pretty much everything. For townhouses and condos, it's the parts of your unit that are not considered common areas. Those common areas are covered by the homeowners' association policies.

Your lender may require that you pay for your first year of coverage and present a paid receipt up front. Some lenders may include it in closing costs, but don't assume this is the case for you. Ask your loan officer. After that first payment, the cost is usually added to your monthly mortgage payment unless you've arranged to pay it separately (but your lender may have restrictions associated with this, so ask). Once you have the details worked out, your coverage will take effect as of the settlement date.

What Does Homeowner's Insurance Cover?

Homeowner's insurance covers the cost, up to the policy limit, to rebuild the house if you experience damage or destruction from an event covered by your policy (a *covered loss*). Some policies, Jonna Wooten says, also may include additional coverage (more on this below). It will not cover your mortgage payments.

You may find that the coverage amount your agent recommends seems lower than you expected. Keep in mind that your home's value is not just the house, but also the value of the land and location it's sitting on. The insurance deals specifically with the house.

In addition to the building itself, your homeowner's insurance will cover things such as:

- *Personal contents.* This can be either a standard percentage of the amount your policy allows for rebuilding the house, or a specific amount you've estimated you would need to replace all of your belongings.

- *Liability.* This protects you in case you're responsible for someone's injury or you damage someone else's property.

- *Additional coverage.* You can add coverage for circumstances not covered in the standard policy. If you're going to live in an area prone to flooding or earthquakes, for example, you can look into coverage for that.

A Question of...Questions

Discuss with your insurance agent what kind of coverage you will need. To help you navigate the conversation and understand what you're getting, insurance agent Jonna Wooten suggests asking the following questions:

- *Is the coverage for my personal property replacement cost or actual cash value?* If your ten-year-old television is damaged or destroyed by a covered event, replacement cost will give you enough to buy a new set to replace it. Cash value will give you only what the old set was worth at the time it met its demise.

- *Does coverage include backup of sewers and drains?* For most policies, this is additional coverage. Discuss with your insurance agent whether you'll need it.

- *Does coverage for the structure itself include the amount stated in the policy, replacement cost, or the stated amount plus an additional percentage?* So what's this all about? Let's say the worst happens. Your house has to be rebuilt, and it'll cost $300,000. Your policy says you get $200,000. End of story? Not necessarily. Depending on the details of your policy, you'd get one of the following (for this example, let's assume the extra percentage is 20%):

Amount stated in the policy $200,000

Replacement cost $300,000

Amount stated plus extra percentage $240,000

That's quite a difference! It sure pays to understand the details of your policy.

- *Are there any special limits or exclusions on the coverage?* The average policy might not cover or may limit things such as valuable jewelry or collections, cash, firearms, and the like. If you need coverage for something that's not included in the standard policy, you might want to ask about adding it.

- *Does coverage include my home business and its property?* You might need extra coverage for this.

- *What discounts do you offer?* Under certain circumstances, your insurance rates can be lowered. Here are a few common discounts:

  - Home/auto, for insuring both your house and your car with the same company.

  - Alarm systems, for increasing the security in your house.

  - Higher deductibles, for taking on more of the risk yourself. Ask for quotes for multiple deductibles to see what fits you best.

  - Age of the home, for certain newer homes with up-to-date utilities. Conversely, there may be an extra charge for older homes with old wiring.

  - Claim history, for a favorable history, if you stay with your current insurance company.

Title Insurance

You have the option of buying title insurance to protect your owner- ship rights. Coverage pays for attorneys to represent you if it turns out that a lien hadn't been detected or your ownership is other-wise threatened. Usually it will even protect you after you sell the house. If you choose it, your title company will arrange for cover-age, and the one-time fee will be included in your closing costs.

While title insurance for you as owner is optional, loan officer Kevin Mahoney says that your lender may require you to get lender's title insurance. This, of course, protects the lender's interests.

15

SETTLEMENT. FINALLY!

My settlement for House #1 was a blur. I remember a room full of people and a ton of papers for all of us to sign and initial and sign and initial...until our hands fell off. And there was this huge sum of *my* money now on the table and no longer lounging in my bank account. One more hour, and the house would be in my possession. But there were all those wretched documents in my way! What if something went wrong? What if someone forgot something? I didn't breathe until I walked out of there with a house in my shopping bag and a folder full of proof that it was mine. Paranoia? Oh, yeah.

Since then, I've been on either the buyer's or the seller's side of the settlement table nine times (so far). The feeling of paranoia eventually went its merry way, but one thing remained the same every time: I was so tired of the whole thing by settlement day that I would have willingly signed away a few years of my life if it meant I could get my new house keys, go somewhere, and take a nap.

Make sure you're prepared to give your home buying experience one last burst of energy on settlement day. Settlement involves a lot of reviewing, inspecting, and signing. You'll probably be pretty worn down after several months' worth of hard work, but you'll have to be observant and alert no matter how tired you are. If you start to worry that you won't have enough time on settlement day to fully review and understand all the paperwork, Associate Broker Susan Corcoran suggests that you ask to see the forms a couple of days before the big day so you can review them at your leisure. They probably won't have your final papers available yet, but you can at least get acquainted with the forms.

The Walkthrough

On the day of settlement and before the meeting, you'll meet your agent at the house for a *walkthrough*—a final review of the condition of the house. The seller should have already moved out, and the house should be empty, clean, and in the condition agreed to in your final contract. There shouldn't be a new hole in the wall of the second bedroom, that old refrigerator in the garage that you said you didn't want should be gone, and the water should flow when you turn on the kitchen faucet. Anything that was supposed to be left with the house (appliances, owner's manuals, garage door openers, etc.) should be there. Repairs required in the contract should have been completed.

If you find any problems, note them for discussion in the settlement meeting. If the problems are big enough that you're not sure you're ready to take possession of the house, discuss your concerns with your agent and attorney.

Final Curtain Call: The Settlement

Around the settlement table will be several people: you, your real estate agent, the seller, the seller's agent, the title agent, and if you have them, your attorney and the seller's attorney. If you cannot attend, the person assigned your power of attorney will act on your behalf. The same applies if the seller is unable to attend.

Identification. Before you begin, you'll be asked to show some form of picture identification, as explained in the letter you got from the title company.

Disputes. If there are any problems between you and the seller, they will have to be resolved. Work with your attorney and agent. Lilian Rodriguez, title agent and attorney, says that the title agent can act as a mediator, but will tell neither you nor the seller what to do. This can end in several ways:

- If you can't resolve the issue, settlement may be canceled.

- The seller can agree to either fix the problem or put money in an escrow account (arranged by the title company) so that you can get it fixed.

- Any new agreements will be included in a detailed contract for you and the seller to sign.

Forms and Signatures. Assuming disputes, if any, are settled, the title company representative will give you a copy of the *Settlement Statement* (also called a *HUD-1*) and additional forms. Review them carefully, especially the filled-in areas and the forms that address your loan. Ask questions if there's anything you don't understand. The seller will do the same. If all is well, you and the seller will sign the forms. There may be additional forms, depending on the state. Again read each one carefully before signing.

The Money. Lilian Rodriguez says that the following will be in escrow, ready for payment:

- Your deposit (earnest money)

- Your mortgage loan

- Money for dispute resolution, if necessary

- Money paid to the seller to pay off their mortgage

- Credit for property taxes the seller already paid for days beyond the settlement

Money left over from your transaction, if you brought more than you need for closing costs and down payment, will be paid back to you after settlement.

Settlement Statement (HUD-1)

The star of your meeting is the **Settlement Statement**. It's a summary of your transaction—who's buying, who's selling, who's providing the mortgage, who's acting as power of attorney (if necessary), how much everything costs, and who pays and gets paid what. Review this form carefully before you sign, and ask questions if there's anything you don't understand. Remember that the dollar amounts may be different from the good faith estimate you received earlier, so again, ask if you need clarification.

The form is divided into two columns, one for the buyer, one for the seller. In each column is a detailed list of items each party is paying for and how much each item costs.

In the buyer's column are the sale price and closing costs you must pay (covered in Chapter 13) and your funding sources. At the bottom is the amount you owe that day to complete the transaction—that big check burning a hole in your wallet.

In the seller's column is a list of money going to the seller (sale price, reimbursements for taxes and other fees paid in advance, etc.) and money the seller owes (such as real estate agents' commissions, mortgage payoff, any payments to the buyer as stated in the contract). Anything left over will be paid to the seller.

It's Yours!!

And now it's time to fork over your down payment and closing costs check. Bid it farewell; it's on a mission. Once all the papers are signed and disputes are settled and money has landed in the right buckets, you will officially become the owner of *Your House.* A round of congratulations will ensue and, more importantly, the keys (*the keys!*) will slide across the table into your waiting hands. Thank everyone profusely for everything, grab your new keys, and go *home!*

16

AFTER THE PARTY

The first time I walked into House #1 after it officially became *my* house, I was overwhelmed with the urge to hammer a nail into a random wall. Just because I could. If I wanted to, I could leave the front door wide open, heating the whole town. I could leave all the lights on. Paint the walls something other than white and put in a carpet that wasn't beige. Because it was *my* house.

So you're a homeowner, maybe for the first time. You have an empty house, and somewhere out there is a van full of your stuff. Congratulations!

Now what?

If you're lucky, you've arranged for the movers to deliver your things right after the settlement. If not, you'll either stay elsewhere temporarily or toss some wood in the fireplace, toast marshmallows, and camp out in your empty house. Hey, whatever works!

As you begin your ownership, there are some things you'll need to take care of early on and some things that you'll find are different from renting if you're owning for the first time. Here are a few.

Settling In

At some point, when you can get your hands out of the endless supply of boxes and packing paper, there are a few things you'll need to remember to take care of. Your real estate agent can help point you in the right direction.

- Change your driver's license to reflect your new address. If you're lucky, you'll get a good picture this time.

- Change your voter registration. You'll need a new card and voting location.

- Register your kids in their new schools.

- Give your new address and phone number to your creditors. It's best if you do this voluntarily.

- Find out when the trash and recycling are picked up and when you can put yours out.

- Choose local service providers: doctor, dentist, veterinarian, mechanic, and others.

- Find the local post office, supermarkets, cleaners, and other stores. If you have teenagers, drop everything and immediately find the nearest mall.

- Give copies of your keys to the people who need them.

One important note about keys: You may want to have your locks changed. Okay, so prior owners usually don't sneak back in to rearrange your furniture. But it's possible that at some point the prior owners misplaced a key, and that key is still out there somewhere. Even if you went the new construction route and there were no other owners, there can be extra keys floating around—and a master key that opens the front door to every house in the development. A lot of people had to get in and out of your newly constructed house before you took possession. If you get the doors rekeyed, all those other keys will be useless, and you'll know exactly who can get into your house.

One last bit of settlement business will happen several weeks after the big day. Once the title company records your title with the state and local governments, you'll receive your title insurance policy and the deed to your new property. Keep these in a safe place!

Protect Your Investment

Several years ago, on the first cold day of the season, I turned on the heat. I heard it click, but no heat came out. Bad, bad sign. After putting on an extra sweater, I made an ever-so-urgent phone call and learned that no one could get to my house until the next morning. (Yeah, I know! And I was lucky they could get there that soon.) When the repair man arrived, he discovered that a part in the heating unit needed to be replaced. Had I gotten the heating unit inspected before the cold weather kicked in, I wouldn't have had to spend the night on my friend's sofa.

You've just spent a huge chunk of your own time, money, and emotions on your new purchase. It may be your biggest investment. So don't let up now! Keep your house and its value healthy with constant maintenance. Not sure how to go about that? Ask your home inspector for recommendations about what kind of maintenance you'll need. Don't wait for something to fall apart. Make maintenance a part of your routine and budget. It'll save you money, time, and stress later.

The Landlord Replacement Kit

If you've been renting until now, it's time to get used to doing some things on your own or hiring someone to do them for you.

You now need a few new things at the ready. You need a Landlord Replacement Kit!

- *A tool set.* These vary in complexity depending on your personal level of handiness.

- *A snow shovel.* If you're graced with an annual winter, you'll need at least one. If you opted for a big plot of land all your own, you might need something more elaborate.

- *Lawn care equipment.* If you're responsible for the land outside, you'll need a few things: tools to cut grass, rake leaves, trim hedges, and other fun things.

- *A stepladder or stepstool.* The first rule of homeownership is that anything that needs fixing, adjusting, or retrieving will be well above your head.

- *Duct tape.* Eventually something in your house will need duct tape. Just last week I used some to patch a small hole in a garbage bag. Yes. I am a genius.

- *Products that seal, loosen, tighten, patch, or de-squeak things.*

- *A home maintenance book.* There are plenty of good books available for homeowners of every skill level, and you might be surprised at how easy it is to fix or maintain some things.

- *The location of the nearest home improvement and hardware stores.*

- *The phone numbers for a reputable handyman, plumber, heating and air conditioning service, electrician, and the like.* There's a service for everything. You'll never have to lift a finger if you have…

- *A checkbook.*

Now don't get too happy and use or do something you don't know how to use or do properly and safely. Ever see those emergency room reality shows? Ouch, ouch, *ouch!* Right. Know your own limits. Hire a professional to do the rest. Personally, I would not touch electrical projects with a ten-foot, nonmetal pole. And I did have to learn my lesson the hard way once when I spent a weekend lifting and moving heavy, stubborn things. That particular flash of brilliance cost me a week of hobbling around with my back shaped like a question mark.

Oh, and while we're on the subject, don't be surprised if, instead of the things you normally get for holidays or birthdays, you start getting house-related things. One year for Christmas, I got a ladder. I'm not joking. Yes, I use it. Stop laughing.

A Loan Again

Over the years, as you bask in the glow of homeownership, you might find reason to seek a new loan or refinance a loan you already have. Here are two that apply to homeowners.

Home Equity Loan. With a *home equity loan*, you borrow money using the equity in your house as collateral. Before you take this on, understand how this will affect your overall financial plans and credit. Can you handle the additional debt? Are there other ways to pay for what you need? Are you willing to risk your house? That's right. You can lose your house if you default on the loan.

And by the way, how much do you know about the lender? The terms of the loan may sound great, but can you trust the lender? Is there any fine print? Find out everything you can about the lender's reputation and the details of the loan before you sign anything.

Refinancing. As we discussed way back in Chapter 5, mortgage interest rates change frequently—sometimes quite dramatically. In the years when interest rates drop considerably, we usually hear a lot about *refinancing*—replacing your current mortgage with another that has more favorable terms. For example, someone with a higher interest rate might want to try for a lower rate.

Someone with an adjustable rate loan might want to convert that loan to a fixed rate. Refinancing can mean lower monthly payments and thousands less in interest over the years.

There are costs involved in the process, though, so you'll need to find out whether it's worth it. Your lender and financial advisor can help you work that out. And if the refinancing lender isn't the one you're using for your current mortgage, don't forget to do your homework and find out what you can about them and the loan they're offering before signing anything.

They Found You!

When you buy your house, the transaction becomes public record. It won't be long before businesses of all kinds come running after you to offer you services, whether you need them or not. As with just about anything else in the world, don't assume that all of these offers are as they seem.

You may receive in the mail a letter stating that you, Mr. and Mrs. Smith, have a mortgage of $200,000 (yes, they know the exact amount). They may offer you the opportunity to refinance or promise you a home equity loan with amazingly low rates or some other incredibly desirable features. Someone else might offer to buy your house, claiming to save you the trouble of going through all the steps in the selling process. Sound too good to be true? It just might be. What do you know about the people making the offer? What's in the fine print? And do you even need what they're offering? Be very careful, because predatory practices abound with these kinds of offers. Work only with lenders and others you know and trust.

Where Did That Lender Go?

Sometimes lenders sell their active loans to another company. That may include your mortgage. Years after you buy your house, you may suddenly get a letter from the current or new lender informing you that your loan now belongs to a new company. The terms of your loan may not change as a result of this transfer, but you'll be sending your payments to someone else from then on. If you're not comfortable with what you see, contact the lenders and ask questions. In fact, contact the original lender to make sure it's a legitimate sale. Scams do happen sometimes.

While you're at it, check with your new lender to verify that they have taken on your tax and insurance payments (the "T" and last "I" in PITI) if these are included in your mortgage payment. If the new company has overlooked these items, your tax authority and insurance company won't know where to send your bills. You don't want these payments to be missed because of an administrative oversight.

Home Base

So it seems we've reached the end. You're armed with the basics, and you're ready to roll. You have a lot of tough decisions ahead of you. I hope this book has helped you pull together the information and people you will need along the way. While this book is a good start, remember there are experts out there, ready to guide you every step of the way. But the more knowledgeable you become, the more effectively you can work with your team. Information like the topics covered in this book can help you anticipate what's coming next.

Whether you're buying for the first time, you're in House #5 like me, or you're in a different house every year, there's something new about every buying experience. Some hit snag after snag, while others run like clockwork. Most are somewhere in between, leaning more toward one end or the other. When you're buying something as important as a house, you never know what excitement lies in store. But if you do everything you can to prepare yourself and surround yourself with the right professionals, you stand a better chance of avoiding at least some of the pitfalls that come your way.

When it's all said, signed, and done, enjoy your new home. Add your own personal touches. Keep the kids from sliding down the banister. Hang something on the wall. Invite your friends over for dinner. After all, it's yours.

Welcome home!

APPENDIX:
CHART ATTACK!

In the following charts record your information as prompted in the chapters. While Charts A through D are not "official" financial forms, they're there to help you start organizing, planning, and thinking about your specific needs. Use them as starting points for discussion with your financial advisor.

Charts E through G will help you figure out what you want in a house and organize your house hunt. Show them to your real estate agent to help him or her understand what you're looking for.

Chart A: Monthly Income

Chart B: Monthly Budget

Chart C: Money You Need Up Front

Chart D: Money Sources

Chart E: Wish List—House Types

Chart F: Wish List—Musts, Wants, Nice-to-Haves, and Nevers

Chart G: Wish List Comparison

Chart A: Monthly Income

Fill in your monthly income from all sources.

Salary/Wages	_____
Bonus	_____
Commission	_____
Overtime	_____
Investments	_____
Child Support	_____
Alimony	_____
Rental Income	_____
Anything else?	_____
_____	_____
_____	_____
_____	_____
_____	_____
_____	_____
_____	_____
_____	_____
TOTAL	_____
36% of TOTAL*	_____

rule of thumb for debt payments, including housing

28% of TOTAL*	_____

rule of thumb for housing payment alone

* Your lender may use different percentages for you; it depends on the shape of your finances at the time you apply.

Chart B: Monthly Budget

A starting point for a discussion with your financial advisor.

Fill in your current expenses and the expenses you will have when you move to your new house. If needed, use estimates for the new expenses, and replace them with actual information as it becomes available.

	Current Budget	New Budget
HOUSE		
Rent/Mortgage		
Homeowner's Association Fees		
Utilities:		
Fuel		
Electricity		
Water		
Maintenance/Improvements		
Emergency Fund		
Cable/Satellite		
Telephone(s)		
Anything else?		
NON-HOUSE		
Food		
Savings		
Credit Cards		
Loans		
Car		
Retirement		
Education		
Childcare		
Child Support/Alimony		
Taxes		

	Current Budget	New Budget
NON-HOUSE (con't)		
Insurance		
Cell Phones		
Clothing		
Vacation		
Entertainment		
Anything else?		
TOTAL		

How does this compare to your income in Chart A?

What's the most you can afford to pay every month for mortgage and related expenses?

Chart C: Money You Need Up Front

Fill in the money you need before or on the day you buy your house. Start with estimates, and put in actual amounts as they become available. You can often get estimates from your real estate agent or loan officer.

	Estimate	Actual
Down Payment	_____	_____
Deposit/Earnest Money	_____	_____
Points	_____	_____
Other Closing Costs	_____	_____
Home Inspection	_____	_____
Moving Expenses	_____	_____
Appraisal Fee*	_____	_____
Anything else?	_____	_____
_____	_____	_____
_____	_____	_____
_____	_____	_____
TOTAL	_____	_____

* if you have to pay it up front

Chart D: Money Sources

What's the maximum amount of cash you can come up with?

Savings	_____
Retirement	_____
Points	_____
Sale of House	_____
Gift	_____
Loan	_____
Anything else?	_____
_____	_____
_____	_____
_____	_____
TOTAL	_____

How does this compare to the amount you need in Chart C?

Chart E: Wish List—House Types

What kind of houses meet your needs? What are you willing to consider? Select the items that apply, and add any notes that will help you round out your thoughts.

1. What's your primary reason for buying?
   _____ Long-term family home
   _____ Temporary place to stay
   _____ Investment you can live in
   _____ Anything else? _____

2. How long do you think you'll stay there?
   _____ Less than 5 years
   _____ 5-10 years
   _____ 10-15 years
   _____ Indefinitely

3. What kind of location will you consider? (circle all that you'll consider)

   Setting: urban / suburban / rural

   Proximity to:
   Neighbors   close / some distance / far
   Work   close / some distance / far
   Schools   close / some distance / far
   Public Transportation   close / some distance / far
   Entertainment   close / some distance / far
   Shopping   close / some distance / far
   Anything else?

   _____   close / some distance / far
   _____   close / some distance / far

   Noise level: quiet / some noise OK / busy area

4. What kind of house will you consider? Mark all that apply.
   _____ Single family   _____ New construction
   _____ Townhouse   _____ Resale - no work needed
   _____ Condominium   _____ Resale - minor/cosmetic work
   _____ Plot of land   _____ Resale - major work

Chart F: Wish List—Musts, Wants, Nice-to-Haves, and Nevers

Mark your preferences. Add items at the end of the chart if needed.

	Must	Want	Nice-to-Have	Never
HOUSE TYPE				
Total square footage:				
Minimum:				
Maximum:				
Age of home:				
Minimum age:				
Maximum age:				
Number of levels				
Exterior:				
Brick				
Siding				
Stucco				
Wood				
Yard:				
Front				
Back				
Fenced				
Land (acres:)				
Surroundings/view				
Lot:				
Cul-de-sac				
Corner				
End unit (townhouse/condo)				
Other:				
Parking:				
Garage (# of cars:)				
Automatic garage door				

	Must	Want	Nice-to-Have	Never
HOUSE TYPE (con't)				
Carport				
Assigned parking spaces				
Unassigned parking				
ROOMS				
Bedrooms:				
Minimum #				
Maximum #				
Bathrooms:				
# of full baths				
# of half baths				
Kitchen:				
Galley				
Eat-in				
Home office				
Formal dining room				
Family room				
Basement:				
Finished				
Unfinished				
Walk-out				
Attic:				
Finished				
Unfinished				
Storage area				
Laundry room				

	Must	Want	Nice-to-Have	Never
FEATURES				
Open floor plan				
Heating:				
Gas				
Electric				
Heat pump				
Forced air				
Central air conditioning				
Fireplace:				
Wood burning				
Gas				
Flooring:				
Carpet				
Hardwood				
Other				
Appliances:				
Washer/dryer				
Refrigerator				
Range/oven (gas or electric?)				
Garbage disposal				
Microwave				
Ceiling fan				
Skylight				
Security system				
Walk-in closets				
French doors				
Recreation facilities				
Clubhouse/recreation room				
Tennis				
Golf				
Pool				

	Must	Want	Nice-to-Have	Never
FEATURES (con't)				
Exercise equipment				
Anything else?				

Chart G: Wish List Comparison

List your Musts and Wants in the first column. Then compare your favorite houses with this list.

Musts & Wants	House 1	House 2	House 3	House 4

NOTES

Chapter 3. Where Credit is Due

[1] The Fannie Mae Foundation and the National Endowment for Financial Education, *Knowing and Understanding Your Credit*, 2002, p.20.

[2] The Fannie Mae Foundation and the National Endowment for Financial Education, *Knowing and Understanding Your Credit*, 2002, p.21.

Chapter 5. Dial "M" for Mortgage

[3] The Federal Reserve Board and the Office of Thrift Supervision, "Consumer Handbook on Adjustable Rate Mortgages," 1997, p.14.

Chapter 6. The Paper Chase: Mortgage Applications

[4] The Fannie Mae Foundation, *Borrowing Basics: What You Don't Know Can Hurt You*, 2003, p.2.

INDEX

YOUR THOUGHTS